House Beautiful
FABRICS FOR YOUR HOME
340 DESIGNER FAVORITES

JENNIFER BOLES

House Beautiful
FABRICS FOR YOUR HOME

340 DESIGNER FAVORITES

JENNIFER BOLES

HEARST BOOKS

A division of Sterling Publishing Co., Inc.

New York / London
www.sterlingpublishing.com

Every effort has been made to ensure that all the information in this book, including fabric names, materials, manufacturers, and colors, is accurate. However, due to challenging printing conditions, some textiles physical appearance will look different than replicated in *Fabrics for Your Home*. The publisher cannot be responsible for any losses and/or other damages that may result from the use of the information in this book.

Library of Congress Cataloging-in-Publication Data

House beautiful fabrics for your home : 340 designer favorites / edited by Jennifer Boles.
    p. cm.
  Includes indexes.
  ISBN 978-1-58816-741-5
  1. Textile fabrics in interior decoration. I. Boles, Jennifer. II. House beautiful. III. Title: Fabrics for your home.
  NK2115.5.F3H68 2010
  747'.9--dc22

                                                                                              2009033784

10 9 8 7 6 5 4 3 2 1

Published by Hearst Books
A Division of Sterling Publishing Co., Inc.
387 Park Avenue South, New York, NY 10016

House Beautiful is a registered trademark of Hearst Communications, Inc.

www.housebeautiful.com

For information about custom editions, special sales, premium and corporate purchases, please contact Sterling Special Sales Department at 800-805-5489 or specialsales@sterlingpublishing.com.

Distributed in Canada by Sterling Publishing
c/o Canadian Manda Group, 165 Dufferin Street
Toronto, Ontario, Canada M6K 3H6

Distributed in Australia by Capricorn Link (Australia) Pty. Ltd.
P.O. Box 704, Windsor, NSW 2756 Australia

Manufactured in China

Sterling ISBN 978-1-58816-741-5

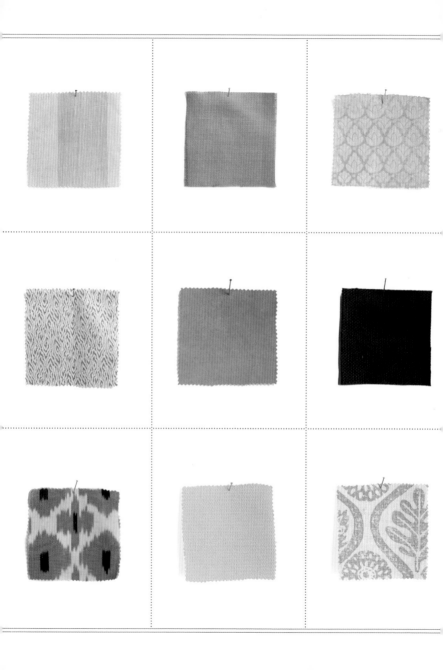

CONTENTS

INTRODUCTION

Why is it that some of us can juggle career and family with aplomb, master the art of French cooking with finesse, and comprehend Proust and his madeleines, yet when it comes to choosing fabrics for our homes, our knees turn to jelly? It's a lot trickier than the decisions we're faced with on a daily basis: Paper or plastic? Regular or decaf? Booth or table?

Perhaps the dilemma lies in the number of fabrics from which to choose. There's cotton, the workhorse of the design world that's appropriate for curtains, upholstery, tablecloths, even lamp-shades. (No wonder it was a favorite of design legend Billy Baldwin.) Silk is nice for window treatments or pillows, but beware this delicate fabric on high-traffic furniture. Linen is always chic and perfect for cool, breezy rooms, but if you are allergic to wrinkles, it might not be for you. And chenille? Children and pets are no match for this durable fabric, something to remember when

In her Ojai, California home, designer **KATHRYN M. IRELAND** went for a brilliant mix of color and pattern. Color-saturated fabrics pack a bold punch in her guest bedroom: The bed-spread and pillowcases with suns are from her latest collection, Sun in Pink. The bolster pillow is made from an antique suzani.

you want your sofas and chairs to wear like armor and stand up to little hand and paw prints.

Another consideration is pattern. Of course, solids are easy to work with, but a room with all solids and no pattern makes for a dull room. (Insert texture in place of pattern and the same rings true, but we'll get to that in a minute). There are stripes, checks, plaids, dots, damasks, florals, geometrics, animal prints, and trees of life. It's enough to make one tongue-tied and bleary-eyed! Let's say you pick a solid for your sofa and a floral print for your draperies (in the same or complimentary color family, mind you). Inevitably, you end up feeling like an old pro. But don't rest on your laurels; you still have some work to do. What about the pillows on your sofa? Are you going to be safe and stick with yet another solid? Or are you going to take a walk on the wild side and go with an animal print? And how about that ottoman coffee table in front of the sofa? A stripe? A plaid?

But let's not stop there. Here's where texture comes into play. Are you feeling sporty? Maybe you want to use a ribbed fabric (think corduroy). Want some sheen? How about a glazed cotton? Need something rustic for your Belgian-inspired home? A nubby linen in a neutral color might

In this den by designer **TOM SCHEERER**, bold concentric circles of a custom braided-wool rug play up the curves of twin bergères à la reine in a blue **H**inson linen. Curly Mongolian lamb's wool covers an ottoman, and the striped sofa is in Jane Shelton Staten ticking with pillows in a **R**aoul **T**extiles floral, **S**ecret **G**arden.

Lively patterns and a mix of seating give this dining area an informal look and sense of fun. **PATRICIA HEALING** and **DANIEL BARSANTI**, with the help of their senior designer **CHRIS DESMONE**, covered a generous banquette in Sari Majolica by Raoul Textiles and paired it with shield-back chairs upholstered in far-from-traditional leather.

be just the thing. And this brings us to that other consideration: color. Color is one of the most important components to the fabric conundrum. After all, isn't color the first thing you see when you walk into a room?

So, after that litany of questions and all the decisions you face, it's no wonder that choosing fabrics can be a very daunting task. What are we to do? *House Beautiful* heard those cries of despair and enlisted top designers to share their wisdom with us, the reader, in the "Instant Room" column. In each column, a designer takes us through the decision making process, explaining why certain fabrics and prints work well together. (Who knew that one room could handle a plaid, a floral, and an animal print—and that they look divine together?) Each designer chooses a master fabric, and then lists numerous options of solids and prints that would work with their selection, leaving the ultimate decision up to us. The fabrics that you choose are almost like answers to a multiple choice question—but no answer is incorrect. Sounds like the odds are in our favor!

Because "Instant Room" has proven to be so popular, the editors decided to compile the column's nuggets of wisdom into this handy guide to decorating with fabrics and prints. You'll also find designer projects that have graced the pages of *House Beautiful*, plus a helpful reference section on the fabrics featured in this book.

We hope that this book will give you the knowledge you need to become confident in your decorating, all the while providing you with inspiration to make your house beautiful.

JENNIFER BOLES

House Beautiful Contributing Editor

WHERE TO BUY FABRIC

Many fabrics are available only 'to the trade,' which means the manufacturers sell primarily to architects and interior designers. But there are other options available. Most towns have a decorating or fabric shop or workroom that will place an order for a specific fabric for you. There are new online services that also do the same. We suggest starting on Google by searching "purchase" and the manufacturer's name, or visiting one of the following services.

DECORATI
decorati.com/info/consumers

L.A. DESIGN CONCEPTS
ladesignconcepts.com

DECORATORS BEST
decoratorsbest.com

DECORATIVE BUYING SERVICE
decorativebuyingservice.com

CHAPTER

1

THE NEW
TRADITIONALS

READY TO BEGIN

Selecting fabric can be challenging. Why not begin with your favorite and start from there? Nine experts weigh in.

BRUNSCHWIG & FILS | VERRIÈRES GLAZED CHINTZ IN BLUE/WHITE (75922-04); COTTON

"I fell in love with it when I first saw it in a drawing room in France. I've had it in my bedroom for years." –MURRAY DOUGLAS

LEE JOFA | ALTHEA LINEN PRINT IN CITRON (2000162-23); LINEN

"Even though the pattern has been in the line since 1923, it still looks fresh, clean, and sort of modern. It's a type of design that never goes out of style." –STEPHEN ELROD

ROGERS & GOFFIGON | SHAKER IN BLITHE (92509-05); LINEN

"It's 100 percent linen, and goes on everything. I use it all the time for upholstery, curtains, and pillows. I just finished a huge beach house in it." –NANCY BRAITHWAITE

CELERIE II COLLECTION THROUGH VALTEKZ
RATTLESNAKE IN NATURAL; FAUX LEATHER

"I'm totally obsessed with our faux leathers, the rattlesnake especially. It's indestructible—a lit match is the only thing that hurts this stuff." –CELERIE KEMBLE

**THE ALEXA HAMPTON COLLECTION THROUGH
KRAVET COUTURE** | GREEK KEY STRIPE IN GOLDEN
MERLOT (22285-419); SILK TAFFETA

**"Only if I can say it's *one* of my favorites. It's
a taffeta, and it's really yummy for curtains."**

–ALEXA HAMPTON

. . . .

STROHEIM & ROMANN | STANLEY MATELASSÉ IN IVORY
(8284B-0014); COTTON

**"I like everything about it. It's great on window
treatments and I even like to sleep with it. It's comfortable, it's unobtrusive, it's charming. And it can
be sexy, too."** –JANICE LANGRALL

. . . .

DONGHIA | SHANGRI-LA IN JACARANDA/BROWN; LINEN

**This linen is like a contemporary toile. I have it
on slipcovers and duvets. It's so lightweight, you
can sleep under it or wear it."** –SHERRI DONGHIA

. . . .

KOPLAVITCH & ZIMMER | FUSCARI IN TRUFFLE/CREAM;
COTTON, SILK

**"I never use the same fabric in more than one
project, with the exception of this damask. I
design chairs so that the emblem is on the back,
front, and seat."** –MARINA KILLERY

. . . .

LELIEVRE THROUGH OLD WORLD WEAVERS | VENUS
DOT IN AZALEE (H007470044); SILK BLEND

**"It's a luminous silk blend with a small dot. Very
chic. I use it in every color and I use it on every
job."** –TONY INGRAO

CLASSIC AND MODERN FABRICS

Even the classics evolve. A beautiful original never goes out of style. The modern look tends to be light, loose, young in spirit. Which do you prefer?

DAMASK

Classic
NANCY CORZINE
CORNUCOPIA IN GOLD; SILK

The ball gown of fabrics, formal and luxurious. This floral pattern was formed by the lustrous silk weave.

MODERN
SCHUMACHER | ABAZA
RESIST IN INDIGO; LINEN, COTTON

A bold-scaled print (it's digital!) with an ethnic spirit and a relaxed attitude.

TREE OF LIFE

Classic

BENNISON | DRAGON FLOWER IN ORIGINAL ON BEIGE; LINEN, COTTON, POLYAMIDE

An exquisitely detailed hand-print that reflects Western fascination with exotica.

MODERN

RUBELLI THROUGH BERGAMO FABRICS | CAP D'ANTIBES IN MULTICOLOUR; LINEN

Dreamy and impression-istic like a watercolor—a look made possible by inkjet printing.

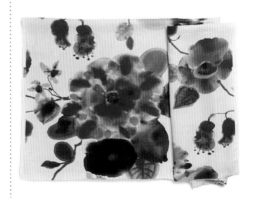

TOILE

Classic

BRAQUENIÉ THROUGH PIERRE FREY | TRAVAUX DE LA MANUFACTURE IN BLEU; COTTON

Toiles tell a story: traditionally it's a pastoral theme in one color (blue, black, or red) on a white or cream background. This one looks like a historical engraving.

MODERN

PIERRE FREY | HONG KONG POSITIF IN LAQUE; COTTON

A Hong Kong student told the story of his city in dynamic sketches that won a Pierre Frey toile competition. Its hand-drawn style captures the energy of contemporary urban life.

HOUNDSTOOTH

Classic

PLACE TEXTILES | BANTRY
CHECK IN HICKORY; WOOL,
NYLON

**Handsome and distin-
guished. Traditionally
wool, the pattern is
a product of the weave.**

MODERN

T4 THROUGH QRNER STR
HOUNDSTOOTH IN MIDNIGHT
BLUE; COTTON, LINEN

**Fresh and fun. Who ever
thought houndstooth
could go coastal? Hand-
printed in the Berkshires.**

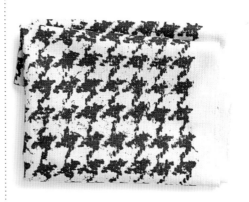

FRENCH COUNTRY

Classic

PIERRE DEUX THROUGH KRAVET BASSECOUR IN FRAMBOISE; COTTON, NYLON, POLYESTER

Tight and tidy, with precisely rendered roosters strutting in rows through a grid of vines.

MODERN

GREY WATKINS THROUGH STARK FABRIC CHANTICLEER IN CHARCOAL; COTTON, LINEN

A feathery blur of motion in freehand strokes, these charcoal roosters are alive!

SUZANI

Classic

DONGHIA | SUZANI IN
PINK PASSION; VISCOSE, SILK,
POLYESTER

**The antique tribal
embroideries of Central
Asia inspired this richly
colored and graphic
woven.**

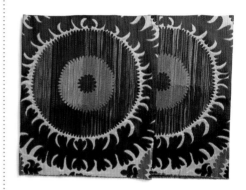

MODERN

**CHINA SEAS THROUGH
QUADRILLE** | SIGOURNEY
IN JUNGLE GREEN ON WHITE;
LINEN, COTTON

**A light and airy look in
lime green that's more
Palm Beach than Silk
Road.**

RIBBONS & ROSES

Classic

COWTAN & TOUT | ORIANA
IN ROSE, BLUE, AND WHITE;
COTTON

**Legendary decorating
firm Colefax and Fowler
filled English country
houses with this sweet
combination.**

MODERN

OSBORNE & LITTLE
COPELAND IN COLOR 03; LINEN,
COTTON, VISCOSE

**Daffodils and silhouettes—
it has the romance of a
19th-century love poem,
with 21st century style.**

FLORAL

Classic

**ROSE CUMMING THROUGH
DESSIN FOURNIR**
DELPHINIUM IN WHITE; COTTON

**One of the most famous
florals by Rose Cumming,
queen of chintz. Aren't
those purples the essence
of femininity?**

MODERN

**ISAAC MIZRAHI THROUGH
S. HARRIS FABRICS** | MEGA
CHINTZ IN CITRUS; LINEN

**An explosion of tangy
colors and big blooms
that bursts with vitality!**

CLASSIC AND COZY

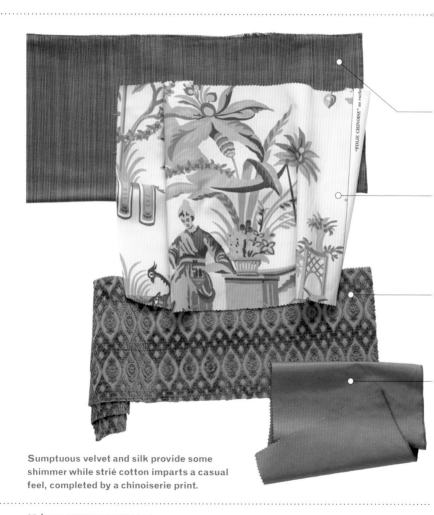

Sumptuous velvet and silk provide some
shimmer while strié cotton imparts a casual
feel, completed by a chinoiserie print.

What's behind the charm of the English country house? Timeless, comfortable fabrics with a hint of refinement. Relaxed elegance is designer **SUZANNE RHEINSTEIN'S** signature, a style that blends traditional and modern fabrics in a cozy living room.

OTTOMAN

"Cover Lee Jofa's Beatrice Ottoman in Covington for a visual exclamation point. It's foolproof for shoes, children, and pets."

CURTAINS & CHAIR

"Showcase the graceful lines and size of Hollyhock's Boone Chair with the deliciously eccentric pattern of Folie Chinoise. Then make curtains from it to bring the color to the walls."

SETTEE

"Hammond is perfect for Lee Jofa's Carlton Settee—a classic pattern on a classic shape—and durable, too."

PILLOWS

"The subtle glow of Glazed Silk makes lovely covers for down-filled pillows."

> *Start Here*

LEE JOFA | FOLIE CHINOISE IN ROSE; COTTON
BEST FOR: CURTAINS AND UPHOLSTERY

" **Use it for curtains, one beautiful chair, and nothing else. Then pull the individual colors out in cut velvets, glimmery silks, and wonderful cottons. Take the whole look down a notch with a sisal rug and you have a young, marvelous room.**"

+ *Silks* ADD ONE FROM THIS CATEGORY

LARSEN THROUGH COWTAN & TOUT | SERENITY IN AZURE; SILK, WOOL
BEST FOR: CURTAINS

A double-sided fabric like this lets you show off the front and back, perfect for unlined curtains.

. . . .

LEE JOFA | GLAZED SILK IN OCEAN; COTTON, SILK
BEST FOR: UPHOLSTERY

It's glazed the way chintz is glazed, so it has a subtle sheen. It's not flimsy and not too stiff, so it molds well.

. . . .

SCALAMANDRÉ | PROVINCE IN PALE BLUE AND PEACH; SILK TAFFETA
BEST FOR: PILLOWS

A pale stripe like this doesn't shout, it shimmers. Wrap it around bolsters or use it for accent pillows.

ROGERS & GOFFIGON | CODA IN WISK; NYLON, COTTON
BEST FOR: BENCH

It looks like grasscloth, but it's flexible. "I like it for a tailored seat on a bench — it makes a room feel more relaxed."

LEE JOFA | HAMMOND IN OLIVE; VISCOSE, COTTON,
BEST FOR: SETTEE

A cut velvet pattern like this goes well with an oversize print. It lends a classic look that suits new and antique furniture.

LARSEN THROUGH COWTAN & TOUT | CANTON VELVET
IN AZURE; SILK, COTTON, WOOL
BEST FOR: BERGÈRE

The silk content makes this velvet especially sumptuous. It looks particularly good with piping details on a shapely, but not oversize, chair.

LEE JOFA | COVINGTON IN ROSE; COTTON, VISCOSE
BEST FOR: OTTOMAN

You can put up your feet on this durable, subtly striped velvet — or pile on stacks of books.

MARKHAM ROBERTS respects the history of this nineteenth-century Southampton house, but makes it suitable for a young family by updating with casual, yet traditional fabrics. The dominant floral, Claremont's Butterfly in Vert, links the two spaces together and adds an intimacy to the sofa's arrangement.

CLARENCE HOUSE | DAHLIA IN MULTI; LINEN

Roberts upholstered one of the living room's two double-sided sofas in Dahlia, a vintage floral print reminiscent of both the house's age and style.

BRUNSCHWIG & FILS | NORFOLK STRIÉ TEXTURE IN LEAF GREEN; COTTON, RAYON

The two tufted chaises—large enough to accommodate several guests at once—reflect the homeowners' casual lifestyle. The green strié fabric serves as a visual respite from the room's prints, while the contrasting bolsters furnish some decorative interest.

OSCAR DE LA RENTA FOR FONTHILL THROUGH STARK FABRIC | JAIPUR CREST IN BROWN; COTTON

While the contemporary fabric used on the curtains departs from the room's more mature flower prints, it has a big impact and lends a sense of playfulness into an otherwise serious space.

CHELSEA EDITIONS | FRENCH KNOT (2011-01) IN CREAM; LINEN, COTTON

C&C MILANO THROUGH HOLLAND & SHERRY 000332 IN GREY-BLUE/IVORY; LINEN

Bilhuber designed a canopy bed to create a restful room within a room. The creamy, embroidered bed curtain blends with the neutral walls, while the serene blue lining acts as a subtle color contrast.

. . . .

JANE CHURCHILL THROUGH COWTAN & TOUT SHELLEY IN CREAM; COTTON, VISCOSE, LINEN

This crisp and masculine print covers the rooms' walls as well as the bed's headboard and siderails. The crosshatch-patterned fabric looks modern, contrasting nicely with the room's softer, more traditional prints.

. . . .

C&C MILANO THROUGH HOLLAND & SHERRY PIENZA CARCIOFINO IN WHITE NATURAL; LINEN

Although pillows are covered in several fabrics, its creamy beige and blue color scheme maintains the bedroom's harmony.

SMART AND CASUAL

A woodsy floral establishes a spring palette
of oak leaves, sandy linen, shimmery velvet,
and leafy green.

Trying for traditional with a modern twist? British designer **NINA CAMPBELL** created a smart but casual family room with updated prints and relaxing colors.

CURTAINS

"I love Delphine's coarse linen texture and the simplicity of the pattern. I'd use grommets and make curtains that hang straight down in a modern way."

SOFA

"The fact that Amisi has two colors in the weave gives it depth and softness. It works on any sofa, but my Collingwood design is extremely comfortable, and looks classic with a contemporary twist."

BENCH

"Giverny Velvet picks up on the taupe in Delphine. It's a grounding color next to the acidy greens, and perfect for accent furniture." Chopin bench by Nina Campbell.

CHAIR

"I always find it handy to have a stripe in a room, especially to mix with a print. They usually work well together. I see Voluta Stripe on the Tiffany Chair—an add-on for a seating group or an extra dining chair." Tiffany Chair by Nina Campbell.

> **Start Here**

NINA CAMPBELL THROUGH OSBORNE & LITTLE | DELPHINE IN COLOR 01; LINEN

BEST FOR: CURTAINS

" I wanted to design something that was organic, but not a floral. I go for walks in the morning and look at the trees, even the bare ones in winter. Then comes spring, and the leaves are suddenly there."

✚ *Accents* ADD ONE FROM THIS CATEGORY

LELIEVRE THROUGH STARK FABRIC | DIAPASON IN ANIS; POLYESTER

BEST FOR: CURTAINS, PILLOWS

"It's not a real silk taffeta, so you can put it in the window and it won't be damaged by the sun."

NINA CAMPBELL THROUGH OSBORNE & LITTLE

GIVERNY VELVET IN COLOR 03; COTTON, VISCOSE

BEST FOR: ANY ACCENT FURNITURE

"There's something wonderful about a good brown."

COLONY COLLECTION THROUGH SCALAMANDRÉ

RONDO IN LINEN AND STRAW; COTTON, VISCOSE, SILK

BEST FOR: PILLOWS

"The small design and neutral colors coordinate so easily with the other fabrics."

Upholstery THEN ADD TWO FROM THIS CATEGORY

FORTUNY | TAPA IN BROWN AND WARM WHITE; COTTON
BEST FOR: BERGÈRE

"Fortuny fabric is enduring. It's a fantastic piece of history, and always glamorous."

NINA CAMPBELL THROUGH OSBORNE & LITTLE
AMISI IN COLOR 03; VISCOSE BLEND
BEST FOR: SOFA

"Chenielle is always comfortable—and this one looks smart, too!"

NINA CAMPBELL THROUGH OSBORNE & LITTLE
VOLUTA STRIPE IN COLOR 03; VISCOSE BLEND
BEST FOR: PULL-UP CHAIR

"I designed the stripes to be varied, which gives it a bit of an edge."

PIERRE FREY | TEDDY IN OLIVE; MOHAIR, COTTON
BEST FOR: ARMCHAIR

"So lovely and cozy and plush—and who can resist a fabric called Teddy?"

GREAT PLAINS THROUGH HOLLY HUNT | SUMMER
CLOTH IN SEASPRAY; LINEN, COTTON

All of Morgan's clients get blue somewhere in
their homes, so it is only fitting that a sofa and
loveseat are upholstered in this sturdy, solid blue
linen/cotton blend.

. . . .

**CHINA SEAS THROUGH QUADRILLE WALLPAPERS &
FABRICS, INC.** | HAWTHORNE (3015-05) IN SKY ON TAN; LINEN

Hawthorne, a large-scale print, covers the two
club chairs. Its cheery blues and whites make a
graphic exclamation mark in the living room.
"Everyone who walks into this house should feel
good," says Morgan.

. . . .

TRAVERS THROUGH ZIMMER + ROHDE | GRAMMONT
(107133) IN LINEN; LINEN

When you use this much blue, you need to layer
in some brown tones and add creamy colors to the
walls for balance. This zebra print helps stabilize
the room and additionally adds a bit of glamour.

ANNIE SELKE freshens up a Cape Cod house with colors evocative of the sea and sand and lively patterned fabrics.

ANNIE SELKE HOME THROUGH CALICO CORNERS
TARA IN CHOCOLATE; COTTON

A chocolate brown sofa anchors the family room. Its solid, sturdy fabric serves as a classic background, allowing the other striped prints to command center stage.

ANNIE SELKE HOME THROUGH CALICO CORNERS
SEEMA IN BLUEMARINE; COTTON

Selke advises mixing patterns by finding common colors; if colors match exactly, they provide no visual interest. This comfortable armchair's small geometric print, for example, contains every color used elsewhere in the room.

ANNIE SELKE HOME THROUGH CALICO CORNERS
SCRAMBLE IN CHOCOLATE; LINEN, RAYON

Because of the strong patterns in the room, the curtain fabric has a looser, more relaxed print. All of the fabrics give a sense of lighthearted fun, which is no surprise as Selke believes that every room should incorporate something that makes you smile.

COOL GLAMOUR

Shimmery fabrics in shades of icy blues and creams—it's the design equivalent of the cool Hitchcock blonde.

Who doesn't want a little glamour in their lives and in their homes? **NANCY CORZINE** creates a sophisticated bedroom with texture that is soft, soothing, and comfortable.

BENCH
"Lapidary has great texture, perfect for a more tailored look." Richelieu Bench by Nancy Corzine.

DUVET AND EURO SHAMS
"Natasha brings elegance and glamour to the room. I'd love to wake up in this bed!"

HEADBOARD
"Tufted on a headboard, Diamanté looks luxurious and rich." Canton Bed by Nancy Corzine.

CURTAINS
"I don't like curtains that look sad—they should have body and luster and fullness. Traffic has all of that."

▶ *Start Here*

NANCY CORZINE | NATASHA IN AQUA; SILK, LINEN
BEST FOR: DUVET AND EURO SHAMS

" This is a contemporary version of a brocade or damask, with a gorgeous luster. The soft, pale colors are very relaxing and refreshing—and isn't that what you want your bedroom to be?"

➕ *Accents* ADD ONE FROM THIS CATEGORY

NANCY CORZINE | ZHANDARA IN ROBIN'S EGG; SILK
BEST FOR: SHAMS, CURTAIN TRIM

"It has a beautiful sheen, and it's very strong—this is a silk that will not wear out."

NANCY CORZINE | TRAFFIC IN OCEAN; SILK
BEST FOR: CURTAINS

"My favorite plaid! It's a classic taffeta in contemporary, light colors. And both men and women do love it!"

NANCY CORZINE | CHINÉE IN PEARL/BLONDE; SILK
BEST FOR: ACCENT PILLOWS

"Elegant and sophisticated, but not so formal that it looks out of place."

ROGERS & GOFFIGON | SOUSSOUS IN TARN; LINEN, SILK, COTTON
BEST FOR: SOFA

"It's a soft color that works with many shades of blue. The silk gives it sparkle and life."

NANCY CORZINE | DIAMANTÉ IN PALE TEA; SILK
BEST FOR: HEADBOARD

"It's beautiful on a headboard, but I've used it for many things—bed skirt, sofa, chairs, curtains."

ROGERS & GOFFIGON | LAPIDARY IN LAGOON; LINEN, SILK
BEST FOR: BENCH

"Textured, but soft and smooth. I'd use it on the reverse for the welts."

COWTAN & TOUT | MINTON IN AQUA; VISCOSE, COTTON, LINEN
BEST FOR: ACCENT CHAIR

"It's unusual, with exquisite embroidery in one of my favorite color combinations: blue and pale tea."

"This is their little cocoon," says designer **HAL WILLIAMSON** of a couple's romantic bedroom. Shades of blue and purple are cooling water colors for this **New Orleans** home's hot, humid summers.

G P & J BAKER THROUGH LEE JOFA | J0571-3 IN BLUE/AQUA; SILK

G P & J Baker's delicately embroidered silk, used on the duvet and pillows, incorporates all of the client's favorite colors. "Everything is silky and plush," says Williamson. "The duvet and Euro shams and neck roll are all well-filled with goose down." Diamond tufting offers additional dimensions of texture to this opulent bedroom.

HIGHLAND COURT | ROBIN'S EGG IN BLUE ICE; POLYESTER, VISCOSE

The bench's bold print is a graphic exclamation point in an otherwise ethereal room. Because the fabric is blue like much of the room, it harmonizes with its neighbors, but its heavy patterns add a modern touch.

KRAVET | SILK RIB STRIPE (9135-1615) IN SPA; SILK

A glossy striped print graces a chair perched in front of billowing curtains. The soft blue tones impart a subtlety in which the stripes recede into the blue background.

JANE CHURCHILL THROUGH COWTAN & TOUT

TALPA STRIPE IN BLUE AND CREAM; LINEN, COTTON, NYLON

That spunky striped linen blend on the chairs and ottoman proves that one modern accent can take years off of a room. Jane Churchill's Talpa Stripe introduces some vigor to an otherwise tranquil space, and Donovan adds another layer of pattern by upholstering the top of the ottoman in mitered stripes.

RAOUL TEXTILES | TEALEAF IN DELFT; OYSTER LINEN

Raoul Textiles' Tea Leaf in oyster linen is a smart choice for the curtains. Though the print might seem subtle, the repeat and the blue and white colorway give it just enough heft so that it's not overwhelmed by the beefy stripes of the chairs.

SOOTHING COLOR
AND PATTERN

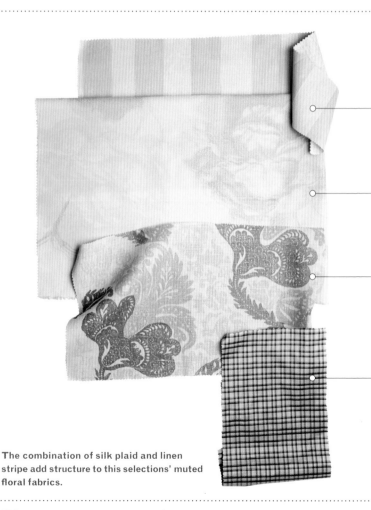

The combination of silk plaid and linen stripe add structure to this selections' muted floral fabrics.

Bold pattern in bright hues imply fun and flirty, but substitute whisper colors and the striking prints become coy and romantic. **BROOKE GOMEZ** isn't afraid to admit she loves pink. Here she selects handprinted fabrics to create a romantic yet formal living room.

CURTAINS

Pompeii Stripe is wonderful for draperies: "Leave the fabric unlined for the beautiful translucency that only linen can give."

SOFA

Rose du Roi, based on an old engraving, covers the Elinor Sofa from the Mariette Himes Gomez Collection for Hickory Chair.

CHAIR

Use Paisley on the Audrey Chair from the Mariette Himes Gomez Collection for Hickory Chair. "It's a sweet chair that needs a fabric with guts."

OTTOMAN

Silk Plaid works well with the box pleats of the Egg Ottoman from Mariette Himes Gomez Collection for Hickory Chair.

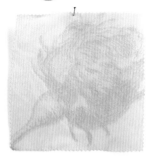

> *Start Here*

TYLERGRAPHIC | ROSE DU ROI IN PLATINUM;
COTTON, SILK
BEST FOR: SOFA

" **The large-scale print has gradations in
pattern and color that make it so soft.
I like to match a fabric with the scale
of the furniture. If everything is loud,
it's not going to work.**"

+ *Printed linens* ADD ONE FROM THIS CATEGORY

TYLERGRAPHIC | PAISLEY IN PINK; LINEN
BEST FOR: CHAIR

Balance the pattern of this delicate linen with a
petite chair frame.

....

KATE GABRIEL THROUGH A.M. COLLECTIONS
ARABESQUE IN FOG; LINEN
BEST FOR: PILLOWS

"I'd take [throw pillows] to the next level by adding
a fantastic metallic fringe."

....

TYLERGRAPHIC | GRANADA IN PINK; LINEN
BEST FOR: CHAIR

Cover a pair of chairs with Granada. Then finish
with a contrasting welt of pink or gray.

TYLERGRAPHIC | POMPEII STRIPE IN LE CIRQUE; LINEN
BEST FOR: CURTAINS

Use Pompeii Stripe to make pretty curtains by lining it with a solid pink linen.

COWTAN & TOUT | MARCO CHECK IN ROSE; RAYON, COTTON
BEST FOR: CUSHIONS

This is a chameleon fabric. "You can use it in a formal way or on seats around a kitchen table."

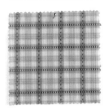

ROSE CUMMING THROUGH DESSIN FOURNIR | SILK
PLAID IN RUBY; SILK
BEST FOR: OTTOMAN

Use Silk Plaid for a great looking ottoman. It really sings with a crisp tailored skirt.

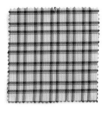

NANCY CORZINE | AMAGANSET STRIPE IN BLUSH; LINEN
BEST FOR: CURTAINS

The vertical nature of this linen makes it perfect for curtains on a tall window.

COLEFAX AND FOWLER THROUGH COWTAN & TOUT
CALDBECK IN BLUE; LINEN

The Colefax and Fowler floral print, used on the vanity skirt and the small bolster, pops as only one of two colors used in this sleepy bedroom. Its aged English look complements the cream and blue wallpaper.

JANE SHELTON | MADISON LINEN IN BLUE; LINEN

The chaise provides a pause from the pattern in the room. Whittaker trimmed the vanity chair in the same blue linen as the chaise, tying the disparate fabrics together pleasingly. The creamy linen of the curtains and vanity chair help to soften things further.

SCALAMANDRÉ | MARA VISTA IN CORNFLOWER BLUE AND CREAM; VISCOSE, LINEN

Whittaker wanted to have fun with the fabrics, so she settled on Mara Vista for the ottoman. The check also appears as trim for the cream shades and on a set of pillows.

For a **North Carolina** mountain house, **PHOEBE HOWARD** selects traditional florals and checks in muted neutrals to reflect the soft-spoken graciousness of this home. A classic check print frames a set of French doors; the earthy color gives the fabric a more modern feel.

GREY WATKINS THROUGH STARK FABRIC | AURORA BELLA IN TAN; LINEN

Howard selected the fabric on these comfortable living room chairs first. The flower motif may seem traditional, but its large scale is modern rather than classic, working well in the soft room.

....

SCHUMACHER | STONE TEXTURE IN ECRU; COTTON

The solid sofa acts as a tranquil contrast to other bold prints in the room and the sturdy cotton. This Schumacher print is surprisingly durable. Limiting the color palette grants this livable room a less-traditional air.

THE COUNTRY LIFE

This arrangement of florals and
faded prints in cheery greens and red is
bound to create a warm, inviting kitchen.

Florals, toiles, checks, and stripes evoke the blissful feeling of being in the country, all without leaving home. Inspired by the radiant French countryside, **KATHRYN M. IRELAND** layers patterns to achieve a European-style kitchen.

CURTAINS
The bigger the pattern, the better it looks in curtains. Try the bold Floral Batik for yours.

ROMAN SHADES
Striped Sheer's crisp linen in red makes for a great window treatment.

SOFA
An abstract floral prints nicely on this George Smith tight-back, scroll-arm sofa.

TABLECLOTH
"There's always someone cooking a quesadilla on the Aga," Ireland says of her own kitchen. Here, she's used a cheery print as a tablecloth for David Iatesta's Provençale table from John Rosselli.

Start Here

KATHRYN M. IRELAND | FLORAL BATIK IN PINK
WITH GREEN; HEMP LINEN

BEST FOR: CURTAINS

**Ireland calls them happy colors. "That
pattern came from an old wallpaper
swatch that I found in a derelict house in
France. But I updated it with that batik
style that I soaked up in Bali."**

Breezy Textures ADD ONE FROM THIS CATEGORY

KATHRYN M. IRELAND | BOUCLE IN RED; COTTON, RAYON

BEST FOR: CUSHIONS

This bright fabric is durable and sturdy. Its nubby,
terrylike quality gives it a casual feel.

CHELSEA EDITIONS | QUEEN ANNE VINE IN WHITE;
LINEN, COTTON

BEST FOR: TABLECLOTH

"It's a fantastic neutral but the crewel work gives it
interest, dimension, and texture that you don't get
from a print."

KATHRYN M. IRELAND | STRIPED SHEER IN RED; LINEN

BEST FOR: CURTAINS

The pomegranate-colored threads in this versatile
linen fabric are deliciously organic.

KATHRYN M. IRELAND | IKAT IN GREEN; HEMP LINEN
BEST FOR: SOFA

Printed on hemp linen, this is at once traditional and modern. It's inspired by old ikat fabrics that are dyed before they're woven, but its floral pattern is abstract.

KATHRYN M. IRELAND | DIAMOND BATIK IN RED;
HEMP LINEN
BEST FOR: CUSHIONS

This hemp linen features layers printed with florals and geometrics, much like Ireland's layered design style.

LEE JOFA | MADELINE WEAVE IN RASPBERRY; COTTON, VISCOSE
BEST FOR: CURTAINS

The tiny scale, puckered texture and sweet flowers of this simple linen make it an ideal accent. "It can be used anywhere in any room because it doesn't overtake anything."

KATHRYN M. IRELAND | GRAHAM IN RED; HEMP LINEN
BEST FOR: TABLECLOTH

Part of Ireland's Batik collection, this sepia-like ground prints on hemp linen.

Although this kitchen seems like it belongs in a French château, it's actually in Houston. Designer **MICHELE ALLMAN** incorporates limestone, aged-looking cabinets, and toile for a setting that could be taken directly out of the French countryside. She selected Bailey & Griffin's Canton Toile 20252 in Cherry Vanilla for curtains and portières (framing the doorway) because of the subtle effect and its subject, a soft pastoral scene.

BRUNSCHWIG & FILS | PAOLA IN PEPPER RED; SILK TAFFETA

The portières (in the foreground) are backed with a checked taffeta. The fabric adds luxuriousness to the toile, and its small pattern complements rather than distracts from the kitchen's simplicity.

BRUNSCHWIG & FILS | LA MER (89756-147) IN POMPEIAN RED; COTTON, VISCOSE, POLYAMIDE

Upholstered in a red wavy print, the kitchen island's stools pop against the green paint, a burst of cherry creating interest and variety against the twelve-foot-long island.

A lake cottage bedroom's quaint fabrics establish a mood that designer **TOM STRINGER** calls fun, easy and simple.

WILLIAM YEOWARD THROUGH OSBORNE & LITTLE
KOTHI IN OLD ROSE; COTTON

The headboard, covered in a traditional, homey print, sets the tone for the rest of the bedding's red and green fabric colorway. Its slightly formal interpretation of a country look helps to tie together the simple furnishings.

LEE JOFA | BELLA TAFFETA PLAID IN CHERRY; SILK TAFFETA

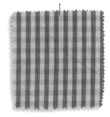

Stringer chose a taffeta plaid for the bed skirt. Despite the fact that the prints don't exactly match, Stringer says it's still cohesive. The coverlet provides some lightness against the colorful fabrics.

FABRICUT | HOLMES IN PEAR; LINEN, COTTON

Throw pillows on beds command attention, but here they impart luster. Stringer's careful selection of fabrics and trims result in lush, green pillows.

SUBTLETY IN THE SPOTLIGHT

Color and pattern prevent creamy linen and muted horsehair from fading into the background.

Subtle fabrics may seem shy, but they're hardly boring. Try pairing them with bolder prints and colors to bring them out of their shells. **WAYNE NATHAN** and **CAROL EGAN** propose a soft take on the study using understated fabrics. The look is sophisticated, not stuffy.

SOFA
Peloton goes on the Palmer Sofa by Roman Thomas. "On a large piece of furniture you want something light," Nathan says.

CHAIR
Biarritz on the Blair Chair by Roman Thomas adds a dose of color.

BENCH
Introduce a graphic element by putting Dreamcoat on Roman Thomas's Dover Bench.

CABINET
To add depth to the Hannover Cabinet by Roman Thomas, upholster the doors with Horsehair I.

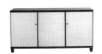

Start Here

ROGERS & GOFFIGON | DREAMCOAT IN RUBEN; LINEN
BEST FOR: CURTAINS

" **As curtains, this pattern goes quiet.
If you're looking for a more graphic
statement, put it on a long bench or
banquette," Carol Egan says of this
stripe. Wayne Nathan adds, "not only is
it bold and graphic, but practical, too."**

Solids ADD ONE FROM THIS CATEGORY

ROGERS & GOFFIGON | PELOTON IN BREAKAWAY; LINEN
BEST FOR: LARGE FURNITURE

This comforting linen makes a versatile background for colorful throw pillows.

. . . .

TWILL TEXTILES | GOOSEYE IN LAKE; COTTON, LINEN
BEST FOR: CHAIR

The pattern of this cotton/linen mix is so subtle,
you can use it like a solid. Mix it with more
pronounced patterns for great effect.

. . . .

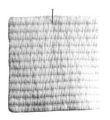

C&C MILANO THROUGH HOLLAND & SHERRY
GIGLIO IN WHITE ISA; COTTON
BEST FOR: ROMAN SHADES

This versatile cotton also works excellently
as upholstery.

Textures THEN ADD TWO FROM THIS CATEGORY

ROGERS & GOFFIGON | BIARRITZ IN FOUNTAIN; COTTON, CASHMERE
BEST FOR: CUSHIONS

Mostly cotton with a touch of cashmere, it's luxurious, but not precious—you can even use it on dining chairs.

· ·

ROGERS & GOFFIGON | BECHAMEL IN MANTIS; WOOL
BEST FOR:

Bechamel, which is 100 percent wool, drapes beautifully for an elegant bed skirt.

· ·

EDELMAN LEATHER | LUXE CALF IN WATERFALLS; LEATHER
BEST FOR:

This glossy leather pairs well with both wood and white furniture.

· ·

ROGERS & GOFFIGON | HORSEHAIR I IN BIRDSTONE; HORSEHAIR, LINEN, SISAL
BEST FOR:

Horsehair I adds dramatic texture. P.S. A little goes a long way.

This Long Island bedroom in cool blues and warm creams, decorated by **DAVID KLEINBERG**, reflects the ocean outside its window.

ROSE TARLOW MELROSE HOUSE | MONTAGUE IN SKY; HEMP LINEN

The faded fabric makes the strong, unusual shape of the headboard (with what Kleinberg calls "wobbly wings") less severe. Kleinberg included nailheads and blue tape trim on the top of the bedskirt, adding definition to the subtle print.

BRUNSCHWIG & FILS | JULIENNE IN STRIPE; SILK TAFFETA

Carefully placed punches of blue appear throughout the room. Kleinberg believes bursts of color create a dramatic impact. The same striped fabric appears on the curtains, only sewn on the bias.

In this South Carolina beach house, designer **JIM HOWARD** creates a modern gathering room filled with antiques and contemporary furniture, hinting at its coastal locale.

ROGERS & GOFFIGON | NEVIS IN MALT; LINEN, COTTON

To Howard, "nothing is too dear or hands-off." While this room is slightly formal, the sofa and club chairs' nubby linen/cotton blend invites casual comfort. A cheery contrast to the dark, cypress ceiling, the creamy fabric establishes lightness and open space.

JASPER THROUGH MICHAEL S. SMITH | TREE OF LIFE IN SAGE; HEMP

The wing chair's Tree of Life print (also used for the throw pillows) introduces a splash of pattern and color. Howard loves all kinds of prints as long as they're right for the situation; to him, most fabrics are appropriate for a beach house—except silk and damask, which are easily damaged by the sun.

THE CLASSICS REINVENTED

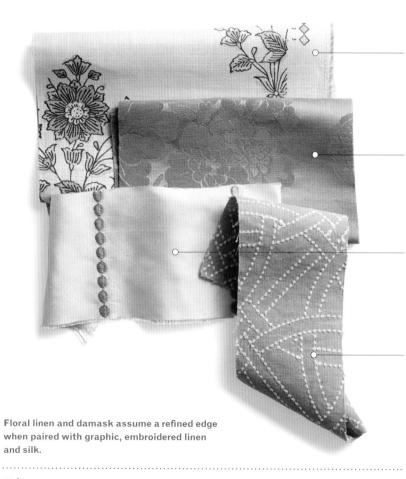

Floral linen and damask assume a refined edge
when paired with graphic, embroidered linen
and silk.

Graphic embroidery? Sleek toile? Take a look at classic fabrics in a whole new way. Traditional patterns inspired by great designs of the past are at the core of a living room designed by **MATTHEW PATRICK SMYTH**.

CURTAINS

"Beatrice Bouquet is a very soft linen that captures light subtly and drapes beautifully. I'd do simple curtains—the simpler, the better—with a bronze rod and rings, or a bamboo pole."

ARMCHAIR

"This isn't a serious, boring damask—it has a lightness to it. Try Pont Royal Damask on a skirted armchair, like the Austin Club Chair from Dessin Fournir."

SIDE CHAIR

"Gabrielle Embroidery is an elegant silk for light upholstery. It should be used on a streamlined piece like the Comédie Chair from Hutton Home, so you see the beautiful lines of the fabric."

SOFA

"The crisp, graphic look of Durance Embroidery bridges contemporary and traditional. It looks best on large upholstered pieces such as the Wingback Sofa from Dessin Fournir."

> *Start Here*

SCHUMACHER | DURANCE EMBROIDERY IN MINERAL; LINEN, COTTON, POLYESTER
BEST FOR: SOFA

" This pattern is based on an antique fabric embroidered with chain stitches. We updated the look so that it feels fresh and new—even a little edgy."

+ *Accents* ADD ONE FROM THIS CATEGORY

SCHUMACHER | BEATRICE BOUQUET IN MINERAL; LINEN, POLYAMIDE
BEST FOR: CURTAINS

"The pattern is a good scale—not big, not small. It has a lot of breathing room. It makes beautiful curtains, no matter what your ceiling height."

. . . .

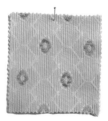

TYLER HALL | CASA DI WHITNEY IN LINEN; COTTON, VISCOSE, ACRYLIC
BEST FOR: PILLOWS

"The medallion effect is pattern, but not a lot of pattern—intricate without being busy."

. . . .

CLAREMONT | TOILE CHENONCEAU IN CRÈME; RAYON, WOOL, SILK
BEST FOR: PILLOWS

"Beautifully woven. I've used it for square pillows with no trim—it's a clean, tailored look."

Upholstery THEN ADD TWO FROM THIS CATEGORY

SCHUMACHER | GABRIELLE EMBROIDERY; SILK, VISCOSE
BEST FOR: CHAIR

"The embroidered beads look like a string of pearls. On a simple wood-framed side chair, it would be a piece of discreet jewelry for the room."

STROHEIM & ROMANN | TANTI FIGURED WOVEN IN AQUA;
COTTON, VISCOSE, LINEN
BEST FOR: BENCH OR OTTOMAN

"A sturdy fabric that's like an updated horsehair. The leaf pattern has a woven tapestrylike effect."

HODSOLL MCKENZIE THROUGH ZIMMER + ROHDE
SILK LINEN STRIÉ IN 955; LINEN, SILK
BEST FOR: CHAIR

"One of my favorites—the color, the subtlety! It's not fussy or pretentious, and works as well on a Billy Baldwin as on a Louis XVI chair."

SCHUMACHER | PONT ROYAL DAMASK IN MINERAL;
LINEN, COTTON
BEST FOR: PILLOWS

This isn't one of your grandmother's formal damasks. It doesn't take itself seriously."

ROGERS & GOFFIGON | MANCHESTER IN BLACK STRAP; LINEN

Gingham is known for being so sweet, so proper, and oh so traditional. Who knew that by blowing up the scale and coloring it in brown and white that gingham could be so…edgy? The print, used on the armchairs, provides a graphic balance and can stand up to the floors.

ROGERS & GOFFIGON | COUNTRY CLOTH IN MOREL; LINEN

To offset the strong pattern in the room, Mitchell chose a cream-colored linen, for the sofa and ottoman, The two neutral elements maintain the soft atmosphere of the room. The embroidered pillows add textural interest to the sofa.

ROGERS & GOFFIGON | SHAKER IN WHEAT; LINEN

For the two wing chairs, it's all about the shape.
Their rustic looking linen is soft like much of the
room, yet the solid fabric allows the chairs' curvy
wings, rolled arms, and fretwork legs to grab
the spotlight.

For his **New Orleans** bedroom, **TOM LANDRY** concocts a contemporary version of Creole décor with a chic and dark colorway of gray, beige, and black.

OLD WORLD WEAVERS | VOYAGE EN CHINE IN BLACK; COTTON, LINEN

Combining toile with luxurious velvet seems so daring and modern, but it's not. Charmed by early Creole settlers who partnered their elegant European fabrics and furniture with more rustic American pieces, Landry mimicks their style with this masculine gray and contemporary beige print.

JOSEPH NOBLE | LUXURIOUS IN ASH; COTTON VELVET

Velvet covers the simple headboard and restrained bed curtains, both of which work well for a man because they're neither elaborate nor fussy. The antique embroidered bed pillows complement the plush look.

A MEDLEY OF PATTERN

Common colors tie these floral, plaid,
paisley, and solid velvets together.

Sometimes, a single print in a room just won't do. Follow **ALESSANDRA BRANCA'S** expert advice as she pulls together stripes and plaids, florals and paisleys, layering pattern in a bedroom that's classic and contemporary.

BED PANELS

Hang the dreamy floral cotton Le Grand Genois Rayure 4 Chemins from the testers of the Barley Twist Bed by Kerry Joyce from Dessin Fournir.

SOFA

Make a graphic yet traditional statement by covering the Reed Sofa from Dessin Fournir with Cecil Wool Plaid.

CHAIR AND BEDSKIRT

Upholster Dessin Fournir's Austin Club Chair with Rajasthan, a richly detailed paisley. Then carry the woven motif through the room by also using the fabric for a bedskirt.

PIPING

Branca suggests quarter-inch piping with Gainsborough Velvet on every upholstered piece throughout the room. Don't forget the bottom of the bedskirt!

> *Start Here*

BRAQUENIÉ THROUGH PIERRE FREY | LE GRAND GENOIS RAYURE 4 CHEMINS IN MULTICOLORE; COTTON
BEST FOR: BED PANELS

" I love the relaxed nature of this meandering floral. It's so versatile, too. I'd use it for windows and bed panels. Pair it with frilly white- or red-striped sheets."

 ## + *Solids* ADD ONE FROM THIS CATEGORY

SCHUMACHER | GAINSBOROUGH IN CHOCOLATE; COTTON VELVET
BEST FOR: PIPING

"Think of piping as an outline that enhances the shape of any furniture."

· ·

ROGERS & GOFFIGON | BECHAMEL IN TSUNAMI; WOOL
BEST FOR: CUSHIONS

Achieve a sense of calm in a room with Bechamel. "The best thing about this fabric is the feminine color on a material, wool sateen, that feels very masculine."

· ·

C&C MILANO THROUGH HOLLAND & SHERRY
MAREMMA IN DARK RED; LINEN
BEST FOR: LAMPSHADES

Make lampshades out of this color-saturated linen. "It's an easy way to dress up a room without being fussy," says Branca.

Patterns THEN ADD TWO FROM THIS CATEGORY

ROGERS & GOFFIGON | TICKING IN VIRGINIA; COTTON
BEST FOR: BED PANELS AND DUVET

When designing bed panels, Branca recommends keeping the interior a lighter color. Use this cotton stripe, and then make a matching duvet to finish the look.

OLD WORLD WEAVERS THROUGH STARK FABRIC
STRIÉ VELVET IN CRÈME; COTTON VELVET
BEST FOR: LUMBAR PILLOW

"Make a lumbar pillow in Strié Velvet—with piping, of course. Then add a red and brown monogram."

LEE JOFA | CECIL WOOL PLAID IN ROSEWOOD; WOOL
BEST FOR: SLIPPER CHAIR

"Mixing organic and geometric patterns is vital to a successful room," says Branca. A plaid like Cecil Wool Plaid will complement a floral.

CLARENCE HOUSE | RAJASTHAN IN RED/BROWN;
COTTON, POLYESTER
BEST FOR: PILLOWS

The intricacy of this cotton/polyester paisley is great for accent pillows and small upholstered chairs.

GREY WATKINS THROUGH STARK FABRIC | RIVIERA STRIPE IN CANNES GREEN; SILK, WOOL

The green silk and white wool striped fabric does not dominate the room because Branca strictly limits the color palette to soft greens and creams. When the light moves through the alternating bands of fabric, it creates another layer of pattern against the walls.

SCHUMACHER | LUCIENNE DAMASK IN PERIDOT; SILK

Cosseting walls are cloaked in green damask, a print that softens the strong vertical lines of the striped fabric. The lavish use of fabric makes for a room that Branca describes as an apple-green jewel box.

COLEFAX AND FOWLER THROUGH COWTAN & TOUT
FLORAL TOILE IN BLUE; LINEN, COTTON

When decorating bedrooms for couples, Roberts doesn't shy away from femininity because he believes "the bedroom is always more about the wife than the husband." Still, this feminine flower motif for the walls isn't too girly.

BRUNSCHWIG & FILS | SCALA METISSE IN 910; COTTON, LINEN

Because the curtains are layered against patterned walls, Roberts settled on Scala Metisse, a creamy textured linen, to take the room down a notch.

COLEFAX AND FOWLER THROUGH COWTAN & TOUT
CHILTERN BOUCLE IN BLUE, CREAM; COTTON

The curvy sofa may appear to be upholstered in a solid, but in fact it's a strié print. The fabric's vertical lines are subtle and do not compete with the room's other patterns.

RALPH LAUREN HOME
CRANE RIDGE TICKING IN BLUE; LINEN

A linen ticking covers the ottoman and provides a dose of masculinity. The fabric also trims the draperies, though the stripes appear diagonally, adding some rhythm.

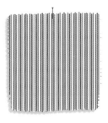

DRAMA

Gutsy prints play the starring role with
a bold black providing contrast. Crewel
fabric and cowhide introduce some texture
to the scheme.

Channel your inner diva with bold prints in even bolder colors. This is not the time to be timid. Follow the advice of **RANDALL BEALE** and **CARL LANA** to create a living room with fabrics that deserve an award for Best Drama.

WING CHAIR AND SOFA
Beale and Lana are wild for pattern. Try the overscale paisley, Distinction, on a Princeton sofa from Lewis Mittman and on the William and Mary wing chair from Lee Jofa.

BENCH
"Hides have a sculptural quality, a texture that adds dimension to a piece, " Lana says. Cover the X-TRA Bench by Edelman in Cavallini.

CURTAINS
"Crewel against black is so dramatic—it just pops," says Beale. With its climbing floral vine pattern, Queen Julie is great for curtains.

PIPING
"Instead of using fringe, outline furniture with piping in the Missoni fabric Zermatt," Lana says.

Start Here

ALEXANDER JULIAN THROUGH STOUT
DISTINCTION IN DOMINO; SILK
BEST FOR: SOFA

" **This silk paisley is a perfect upholstery fabric,**" says designer Randall Beale. " **I see it tufted on a Chesterfield sofa— tons of buttons, big and formal.**"

➕ *Accents* ADD ONE FROM THIS CATEGORY

MULBERRY HOME THROUGH LEE JOFA | PARISIAN SCENE IN BLACK; LINEN, COTTON
BEST FOR: CURTAINS

"I would use it as wall upholstery, and for curtains, too—that whole toile look, one fabric all over, the way the French do it," says Beale.

. . . .

LEE JOFA | QUEEN JULIE IN BLACK; WOOL, COTTON
BEST FOR: CURTAINS

"Queen Julie makes beautiful curtains," Carl Lana says. "And don't be intimidated by the black ground. It adds drama to any setting, casual or formal."

. . . .

CLARENCE HOUSE | VELOURS GASCOGNE IN PIVOINE; COTTON, LINEN, CUT VELVET
BEST FOR: PILLOWS

This accent fabric is perfect for throw pillows or on a pair of chairs.

Upholstery THEN ADD TWO FROM THIS CATEGORY

OLD WORLD WEAVERS THROUGH STARK FABRIC
GARBO IN GRAPHITE; VISCOSE BLEND
BEST FOR: CHAIR

The sturdiness of Garbo makes it just right for upholstery. Beale and Lana also suggest using the viscose blend for piping.

....

EDELMAN LEATHER | BASKET WEAVE IN SWAMP; LEATHER
BEST FOR: OTTOMAN

"I love a leather like Basket Weave for an ottoman," says Beale. "Put your feet up and enjoy. The more beat up, the better. And we'd use nailheads. Tons and tons of nailheads."

....

EDELMAN LEATHER | CAVALLINI IN PEARL GREY; COWHIDE
BEST FOR: BENCH

"Something fuzzy is always nice," says Lana. "The texture of the cowhide adds such dimension. Why not use it for a rug?"

....

MISSONI THROUGH STARK FABRIC | ZERMATT IN
BLACK AND WHITE; COTTON
BEST FOR: PILLOWS

"Zermatt is a great basic fabric," says Beale. "Use it for small- or large-scale pieces, pillows, or welting."

THE NEW TRADITIONALS | **95**

LULU DK | MADISON IN DRIFTWOOD; ACRYLIC

The length of the banquette (ten feet long!) is certainly impressive, and its print makes it even more so. One of the boldest fabrics in the room, "Madison's" bamboo motif, provides graphic contrast to the stripes of the faux painted walls. Jeffers believes the key to marrying pattern is to use different scales and textures.

OLD WORLD WEAVERS | GARIBALDI IN ADRIATICA; ACRYLIC

That large pillow stored in the coffee table is actually a dog bed made from an outdoor fabric, one that holds up well to the homeowners' Labradoodle. The flowery print is a surprise in a room filled with strong, geometric pattern, but the blue and white coloration allows it to blend in.

CLARENCE HOUSE | COTTON VELVET IN BURGHUNDY; COTTON

The headboard, inspired by one designed by Albert Hadley, is grand, whimsical, and over-the-top. The rich velvet only heightens the bed's commanding presence.

CLARENCE HOUSE | MATISSE IN BLACK; COTTON

Because the black and white carpet sets the tone for the bedroom, Shubel chose to maintain the graphic color scheme throughout; otherwise, it would command all the attention. The strong but loose print that covers the armchair balances out the tight pattern on the floor.

CALICO CORNERS | CRANSTON IN IVORY; COTTON

Because of the room's other robust elements, the curtains are clean and classic. Ivory velvet furnishes a note of quiet luxury, and the black tassel trim frames the curtains, tailored and sophisticated.

BALANCING ACT

A leopard print and a floral serve as the spice,
while the metallic chevron and black shagreen
add some sizzle.

Balancing texture, pattern, and color means making sure that all three stay in step—and that one won't get out of line. **LARRY LASLO'S** classic interiors feature a little drama as his signature. Here, he proposes a living room using fabrics with interesting texture, complementary colors, and a few great prints.

CURTAINS
"From Cleopatra to Madonna, the world never tires of leopard—every year a new version comes out. I love it in unexpected colors, like this blue."

CHAIR
Upholster the Pull-Up Chair—designed by Laslo for Ferguson Copeland—in Nurture, a fabric that Laslo says "creates a wonderfully cozy feeling, like you're sitting in a soft bed of leaves."

OTTOMAN
The Directoire Ottoman, also designed by Laslo for Ferguson Copeland, is the right size for an accent fabric like Shagreen. "The embossed leather looks beautiful on small surfaces."

SOFA
"A chevron pattern is simple and easy on the eyes." Upholster a large surface like Laslo's French Deco Sofa in Enthusiast.

> *Start Here*

ROBERT ALLEN | NURTURE IN TIDAL; VISCOSE BLEND
BEST FOR: DINING CHAIRS

" **This is a viscose blend that looks hand-woven,**" says designer Larry Laslo. "**Nurture is soft and homespun—it has what I'd call a lightness of being. It looks great with silk, with things that have luster. I'd use it on a tallback dining chair.**"

+ *Windows* ADD ONE FROM THIS CATEGORY

ROBERT ALLEN | NATURES WEB IN MICA; POLYESTER
BEST FOR: CURTAINS

"I just used Natures Web on top of a blue taffeta for curtains. Don't sew the two together, so you can draw the silk curtains and let the sun shine through the polyester fabric."

ROBERT ALLEN | ELEMENTS IN SEA; RAYON, POLYESTER
BEST FOR: PILLOWS

"The surprise of Elements is the fun of its color." Make pillows out of the rayon/polyester to spruce up a sofa.

JOHN HUTTON TEXTILES | PRECIOUS METAL IN PLATINUM; SILK, LUREX
BEST FOR: CURTAINS

"I would hang Precious Metal as a shower curtain with a liner to give your bathroom a lift."

Upholstery **THEN ADD TWO FROM THIS CATEGORY**

RUBELLI THROUGH BERGAMO FABRICS | PANFORTE
IN COLOR 9; VISCOSE BLEND
BEST FOR: CHAIRS

"I love tweed for the home. The texture of Panforte is great for a pair of chairs. I even see this viscose blend as drapery dressed up with hardware and tapes."

ROBERT ALLEN | ENTHUSIAST IN WATER; VISCOSE BLEND
BEST FOR: SOFA

"You can do a whole sofa in Enthusiast and it won't demand all the attention in the room." It's an ideal backdrop for patterned accent pillows.

JOHN HUTTON TEXTILES | MOBY DICK IN MOODY BLUES;
VISCOSE, COTTON
BEST FOR: SLIPCOVERS

"I always look to a small-scale stripe like Moby Dick for relief from larger patterns."

EDELMAN LEATHER | SHAGREEN IN CAVIAR; LEATHER
BEST FOR: CHAIR

Breathe new life into a favorite chair with Shagreen. "I've covered a Chippendale chair with the leather and it gave a newness to the piece."

Designer **GINGER BARBER'S** assignment
for this Houston home: Marry casual
American style to English propriety by
mingling dressy and comfortable fabrics.

HODSOLL MCKENZIE THROUGH ZIMMER + ROHDE
REGENCY STRIPE IN 503; SILK

Barber chose a muted yellow color scheme for the
living room. The striped floral silk curtains strike
an elegant note, while the subtle pale yellow print
harmonizes with the rest of the room.

DOGWOOD | DAVENHAM IN BISCUIT; LINEN, VISCOSE

Relaxed linen covers the tufted sofa. The casual
fabric serves as a perfect balance to the silks and
taffetas favored by the homeowners. Tapestry pillows, like those seen here, provide great accents
to the big linen sofas.

J. ROBERT SCOTT | MATIGNON IN DOVE; SILK DAMASK

The bench's updated damask holds its own with the more contemporary fabrics in the room. The dove gray colorway is in keeping with the room's sleek personality, while the quiet pattern imbues some femininity to the room.

CLASSIC CLOTH THROUGH DESSIN FOURNIR
MATELASSÉ DAMASK IN MORTAR; COTTON, WOOL, SILK

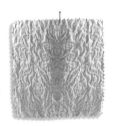

Both the cowhide-covered console and this matelassé coverlet are textured fabrics that beg to be touched. In a neutral gray room, texture can go a long way to add warmth and prevent the room from looking too sterile.

CLASSIC CLOTH THROUGH DESSIN FOURNIR
AUBUSSON IN GREY GOOSE; COTTON, SILK

For the curtains, Ferrier selected a gray, loosely woven solid to allow filtered light into the room. Its simplicity balances out the use of texture and pattern elsewhere in the room.

SPOTLIGHT
ON TEXTURE

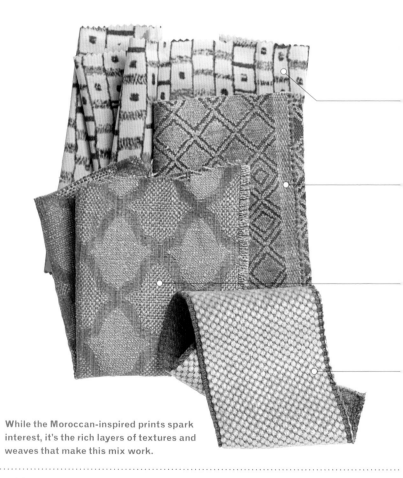

While the Moroccan-inspired prints spark
interest, it's the rich layers of textures and
weaves that make this mix work.

Don't let color and pattern do the lion's share of the work. Sometimes, texture in all of its woven glory can have the most impact in a room. **THOMAS O'BRIEN** designs a living room filled with pale blues and earthy neutrals, plain but luxurious wovens, and Moroccan patterns with a modern take. What could be more fresh?

CURTAINS
"A horizontal wave of blue runs through Calliope, giving it a lyrical spirit. It's fantastic for curtains because it's full of movement but also orderly."

CLUB CHAIR
"Morocco Chenille has an intricate weave that looks great on a club chair. Paolo is one of my favorites—a mid-century shape with a softer sweep to the arm."

ACCENT CHAIR
"The Eliza chair is an oversize lowsitting armchair in oak, extremely comfortable. It's good for a pattern with a bigger scale, like Tamora Weave."

SOFA
"I always want the sofa covered in a restful, simple fabric, because it's the largest amount of fabric in the room. Steed Chenille is subdued, but it's also very rich—perfect for the Tilden Sofa."

Start Here

THOMAS O'BRIEN THROUGH LEE JOFA
MOROCCO CHENILLE IN REEF; RAYON, POLYESTER, COTTON
BEST FOR: CLUB CHAIR

" I based this design on an old Moroccan carpet, paring it down to its essence. I like its spirit, the freshness."

Accents ADD ONE FROM THIS CATEGORY

THOMAS O'BRIEN THROUGH LEE JOFA | CALLIOPE IN OCHRE; SILK
BEST FOR: CURTAINS

"With a large, free-flowing graphic printed on such beautiful silk, you just want to see this as curtains—or a dress!"

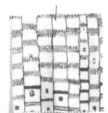

LEE JOFA | NYMPHEUS PRINT IN NATURAL; LINEN
BEST FOR: PILLOWS

"One of my favorites forever! I use it for everything from pillows to panels, and always on the reverse—the print is more abstract that way."

FORTUNY | MELILLA IN INDIGO BLUE AND SILVERY GOLD; COTTON
BEST FOR: PILLOWS

"Magical and timeless, a fabric that's more than a fabric. It's like a fine antique."

THOMAS O'BRIEN THROUGH LEE JOFA | TAMORA
WEAVE IN AEGEAN; RAYON, COTTON
BEST FOR: CHAIR

"A really good textured woven in a chic pattern that works on any kind of chair."

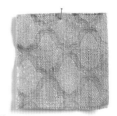

MULBERRY HOME THROUGH LEE JOFA | STEED
CHENILLE IN SAND; VISCOSE, COTTON
BEST FOR: SOFA

"One of my top choices for a sofa. Plain but pretty. The color is perfect."

SCALAMANDRÉ | CORKE LODGE IN GOLD; SILK VELVET
BEST FOR: SOFA

"Another good choice for a sofa. It has an antique quality, a two-tone character that I love."

ROGERS & GOFFIGON | RONDO IN RHYME; LINEN
BEST FOR: CHAIR

"Wonderful sheen and depth. I can see it on dining chairs, an armchair, a sofa."

BEACON HILL THROUGH ROBERT ALLEN | DOVER IN PAPRIKA ; COTTON, POLYESTER

The wing chairs' paisley print, meant to evoke a warm challis shawl, is a classic large-scale exotic print often found often in English interiors. The nailhead trim accentuates the unusual shape of the tall chairs.

KRAVET | MINUET IN HERITAGE GREEN; SILK VELVET

Green velvet curtains are yet another element common to English interiors, though not many can claim to be a tongue-in-cheek ode to Scarlett O'Hara. Lysdahl notes that the room "has an English Regency feeling—sort of genteel, but slightly shabby too."

SCALAMANDRÉ | LEOPARDO IN IVORY, GOLD, AND BLACK; SILK VELVET

In a neutral room, a leopard print pillow becomes graphic, but in a richly layered room such as this, the leopard adds even more exoticism, as if it was imported in directly from Africa.

GRETCHEN BELLINGER | PASHA IN CLARIFIED BUTTER; LINEN, LINEN VELVET

A plump banquette, covered in a taupe velvet, sets the mood for a room where Branca hopes people will walk in and say "*Ahhhhh….*"

ROGERS & GOFFIGON | PARRAMORE ISLAND IN RED; LINEN

Branca loosely drapes ticking over the circular ottoman, perfectly expressing her belief that things don't have to be flashy to be elegant. The fabric acts like a skirt with the soft folds preserving the laid-back atmosphere.

FONTHILL THROUGH STARK FABRIC | CHELSEA STRIÉ VELVET IN GLADE; COTTON VELVET

With a banquette as large as this one, contrasting throw pillows help to define the space. A floral print supplies some color and patterned interest to the sofa, while the soft blue velvet presents yet another sensual layer.

CHAPTER

2

MIXES TO MAKE YOU HAPPY

MOOD LIFTING FABRICS

Paired with a green woven floral, an orange
cotton, and an ikat linen, this peppy fishbowl
print will pop no matter where you put it.

Lift your spirits with these exuberant prints. **MICHAEL WHALEY** believes in boldly colorful rooms and tells his clients to "Go for it!" He suggests a family room inspired by deliciously upbeat prints.

WING CHAIR AND CURTAINS

"I'd make simple pleated curtains with this, and then I'd also use it on the Mrs. Wing Chair. What a fun fabric for a fun chair! Makes me feel like Alice in Wonderland." Chair from Brunschwig & Fils.

SOFA

"Rosamund has an easy elegance that works beautifully on the Westminster sofa, with its classic shape, its simple lines." Sofa from Summer Hill.

CHAIR

"Linen is the right fabric for a family room—relaxed, but also crisp and fresh. For graphic punch, I'd cover a pair of Draycott chairs in Cintra." Chair from Lee Jofa.

BENCH

"Why be bashful? Cover that big tufted Chelsea Bench in electric orange Ottoman!" Bench from Baker.

> **Start Here**

THIBAUT | FISHBOWL IN WHITE; COTTON
BEST FOR: CHAIR

" Fishbowl sets the whole tone. There are goldfish swimming, butterflies flying, turtles crawling, all kinds of things going on. The scale is big, the colors are brilliant. I love those colors!"

➕ *Accents* ADD ONE FROM THIS CATEGORY

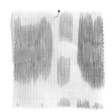

ALAN CAMPBELL THROUGH QUADRILLE WALLPAPERS & FABRICS, INC. | CINTRA IN TANGERINE/JUNGLE GREEN ON TINT; LINEN
BEST FOR: CLUB CHAIRS OR SOFA PILLOWS

"A classic ikat in updated colors. Pillows would give you a little punch, club chairs would be more daring."

. . . .

QUADRILLE WALLPAPERS & FABRICS, INC.
SAN MICHELE IN ROSSO ON BEIGE; LINEN
BEST FOR: SOFA PILLOWS

"They started with a damask and made it groovy— a contemporary, casual look, especially on linen."

. . . .

GROUNDWORKS THROUGH LEE JOFA | DEJI PRINT IN CARNIVAL; COTTON
BEST FOR: OCCASIONAL CHAIR

"What I like is the mix of colors and the huge scale. Use it once."

Upholstery THEN ADD TWO FROM THIS CATEGORY

JANE CHURCHILL THROUGH COWTAN & TOUT
ROSAMUND IN GREEN; COTTON, VISCOSE, LINEN, NYLON
BEST FOR: SOFA

"The woven flower and strié pattern gives a sofa interest without being too busy."

PIERRE DEUX | OTTOMAN IN ORANGE; COTTON, POLYESTER
BEST FOR: OTTOMAN

"For a hot jolt of color. It needs a big piece of furniture to make the orange statement!"

LEE JOFA | INSECARE WEAVE IN CLOVER; COTTON, RAYON
BEST FOR: SEAT CUSHIONS

"An ideal complement to the Fishbowl print. The insects carry on the nature theme—and those little blue wings just jump out at you!"

BRUNSCHWIG & FILS | CHANCELLOR STRIÉ IN JADE;
VISCOSE, COTTON BLEND
BEST FOR: SOFA

"Not everyone wants a floral for their sofa. This snazzy strié is a more modern alternative."

CHINA SEAS THROUGH QUADRILLE WALLPAPERS & FABRICS, INC. | LYSETTE REVERSE (4100-11) IN MAGENTA ON TAN; LINEN

This bright pink cherry blossom pops on the sofa against the saturated blush pink walls and subtle gray and white floors.

CHINA SEAS THROUGH QUADRILLE WALLPAPERS & FABRICS, INC. | LYSETTE REVERSE (4100-03) IN PALM GREEN ON TAN; LINEN

The print on these pillows may look familiar; it's the negative rendering of the same print used to upholster the sofa. Here in Palm Green on Tan, this is a great trick to try if you are nervous about adding a second print to your interiors.

BRUNSCHWIG & FILS | MADHYA WOVEN STRIPE IN ROSE/PISTACHIO; COTTON, ACRYLIC

The crisp green, white, and pink stripes on the pair of armchairs pick up colors from the other upholstery and complement the sofa's bold floral.

RALPH LAUREN HOME | CENTERVILLE TICKING IN LIGHT BLUE; COTTON

The crisp blue-and-white ticking stripe flanks the doorway in an elegant portières. Diamond and Baratta both believe that curtains should always be done in stripes, which helps to add a visual height to the room and windows.

NORBAR | TOBAY IN SKY; COTTON

Pink and blue cotton curtains frame the windows at the back of the room, and those colors are repeated elsewhere as well. Walls, window curtains, and the inside of the portières feature a variety of striped fabrics.

PIERRE FREY | BEAUBOURG 2190 IN DRAGEE 258; TREVIRA CS

The chairs are covered in a solid print, which may have been too potent in a tamer room. It works great here; the bold bright pink color stands up to the other assertive stripes.

COORDINATED COLOR

A citrusy floral twill, blue seaweed-print cotton, and plucky stripes help to create a serene bedroom that is both vibrant and relaxing.

How do you create a carefree room? Try pairing prints in coordinating colors, like **ANNIE SELKE** did here. "It's a restful, serene combo, not as disparate as it might seem because the colors are matched."

CHAISE
Selke puts Starboard Ticking on the 3825-21 Chaise, which is part of the Pine Cone Hill Home Collection by Lee that she designs. She suggests also using the fabric for curtains.

CHAIR
A sweet fabric for a sweet shape, Uma is perfect for the 5089 Chair from Lee. Selke went with Indigo for the bedroom, but "this fabric looks great in every color," she says.

BED
Longpoint goes on the 8605-50 Neo Wing Bed, also part of the Pine Cone Hill Home Collection by Lee. "The color transports you to a coastal destination of your choice!"

CHAIR
On the 1905 Neo Wing Chair, Selke uses Star Crewel. "Its handmade quality adds depth to the room," she says. "This fabric has a good scale. It's not too big so it doesn't overpower."

Start Here

PINE CONE HILL | LONGPOINT IN CITRUS;
COTTON TWILL
BEST FOR: BED

" **I call Longpoint a glorified solid,"** Annie
Selke says. "It's a bold pattern and the
scale seems powerful, but the positive/
negative makes it feels like one color."

 Textures ADD ONE FROM THIS CATEGORY

RALPH LAUREN HOME | MONTGOMERY HERRINGBONE
IN FLAX; LINEN, COTTON
BEST FOR: BENCH

Mixing in a natural fabric is a great way to add a
dose of texture to a casual room.

PINE CONE HILL | STAR CREWEL IN LEAF; COTTON,
WOOL EMBROIDERY
BEST FOR: WING CHAIR

"Often you see a large, meandering design, but
this cotton with wool embroidery is more linear,
so it feels fresh."

SEACLOTH THROUGH LEE JOFA | WOVEN SOLID IN
MIDNIGHT; COTTON
BEST FOR: PILLOWS

Despite its durable look and composition, woven
solid is unbelievably soft.

PINE CONE HILL | STARBOARD TICKING; COTTON TWILL
BEST FOR: CHAISE LONGUE

"Starboard Ticking is an irregular stripe, so it acts as a big pattern. I made all the colors the same intensity, which helps it sit back a bit."

PINE CONE HILL | UMA IN INDIGO; COTTON
BEST FOR: ARMCHAIR

"She's a wonderful, exotic bitsy," Selke says. "This one breathes, it's light, but it does have some *oomph*. Uma knows when to be center stage."

RALPH LAUREN HOME | RYAN STRIPE; COTTON
BEST FOR: OTTOMAN

"There's a place for both irregular and regular stripes," Selke says. Try the very charming Ryan Stripe for an evenly spaced stripe in a smaller scale.

SEACLOTH THROUGH LEE JOFA | SOLID IN PARCHMENT;
COTTON, LINEN
BEST FOR: CHAIR

Sometimes you just need a little breathing room. This cotton/linen mix provides a break from pattern and color.

LARSEN THROUGH COWTAN & TOUT | CINEMA IN KOALA; MOHAIR, COTTON

The pile and sheen of the sofa's mohair may look as delicate as velvet, but according to Smith, it's indestructible. The sofa's luxurious down cushions and pillows envelope you once you sit down. The fabric's warm fuzziness adds textural detail. The wing chair sports one of the most interesting fabrics in the room. The raised, woven leaf pattern acts as a relief against the golden background.

CLARENCE HOUSE | LA MALCONTENTA IN YELLOW/ BROWN; VISCOSE

There is something about ribbed textiles, like that on the bergère, that encourages people to rub their hands over them. The beautiful, timeless fabrics give the room a European feeling. Its embroidered floral print adds depth and coziness to the living room.

This lake house breakfast nook, designed by **TOM STRINGER**, makes for cheery—and comfortable—mornings. Although the fabrics don't quite match, they are all cohesive in a blue, yellow, and white color palette.

JANE CHURCHILL THROUGH COWTAN & TOUT | SAIL
MULTI STRIPE IN BLUE; COTTON

Lacquered fabric roller shades in a strong print dominate, yet its soft blue and yellow colors subdue the strict graphic lines. Its stripes also emphasize the verticality of the windows.

BRUNSCHWIG & FILS | MONTBARD LINEN AND COTTON
PRINT IN LEMON; LINEN

A classic floral imparts a different layer of pattern to the pillow grouping, softening the stripes of the cushion and the shades. A sunny shade of yellow brightens the assortment of fabrics on the window seat.

DESIGNERS GUILD THROUGH OSBORNE & LITTLE
PEAWEED IN INDIGO; COTTON

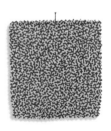

The small, tight print of Peaweed appears on the two central pillows, and reads as a solid from afar. The pillows are trimmed in a contrasting color, extending the use of yellow towards the middle of the nook.

FRESH, SPIRITED TRADITIONAL

Stylized flowers and a graphic stripe are the contemporary yin to the traditional yang of pale aqua linen and cut velvet.

Pick sophisticated, modern prints in clear, vivid colors to update a room without making it look too youthful. "Bedrooms should be about comfort, beauty, and function," says designer **TODD ROMANO**. Here he designs a cozy, bright, and current bedroom with contemporary prints and traditional fabrics.

BED
"The rectangular shape of the Sophia bed lends itself to a strong stripe like Alpha Stripe." Bed from Mattaliano.

BENCH AND SHAMS
"Shams in Large Pansy will pop against the stripe of the headboard. Repeat the fabric at the foot of the bed on a bench. The colors complement each other without being too matchy-matchy." Anthony Bench from Mattaliano.

BERGÈRE
"Think of French chairs as picture frames. You should fill them with something wonderful, like a fabric with movement such as Carnot." Louis XVI Library Chair from Dennis & Leen.

CURTAINS
"There's an elegance in the simplicity of solid curtains. Fiorella has a weight to it that hangs beautifully."

> *Start Here*

T4 FABRICS | ALPHA STRIPE; COTTON, LINEN
BEST FOR: HEADBOARD

" What I love about this stripe is the combination of widths and colors. On one hand it's a strong geometric print, but because of the way it's colored there's a happy, light feeling to it. Linen has the softness and cotton has the strength."

➕ *Accents* ADD ONE FROM THIS CATEGORY

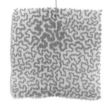

JANE SHELTON | VERMICELLI SQUARE IN BLUE; LINEN
BEST FOR: PILLOWS

"This is what's called a 'ditzy' pattern. It's so simple at first glance, but chic and easy to use."

T4 FABRICS | LARGE PANSY IN DANUBE BLUE; LINEN
BEST FOR: SHAMS OR BENCH

"The flower is feminine and retro, very early '60s. But printed on herringbone, which is tailored and masculine, it becomes quite modern."

CHINA SEAS THROUGH QUADRILLE WALLPAPERS AND FABRICS, INC. | GINZA IN BROWN, CAMEL, AND AQUA ON WHITE; LINEN
BEST FOR: PILLOWS

"Just so happy and whimsical. This fabric makes me smile just to look at it."

Statements THEN ADD TWO FROM THIS CATEGORY

**NORTHCROFT THROUGH TODD ALEXANDER
ROMANO** | ROCHELLE IN AQUA; COTTON
BEST FOR: CURTAINS OR WALLS

"Durable, beautiful. The chicest apartment I've ever been to had this velvet everywhere."

NORTHCROFT THROUGH TODD ALEXANDER ROMANO
FAIDHERBE IN CANTON; COTTON, POLYESTER
BEST FOR: SIDECHAIR

"This fabric is so elegant! I love a cotton velvet, and in a pattern—even better."

ROGERS & GOFFIGON | FIORELLA IN VAN DYKE; LINEN, SILK
BEST FOR: CURTAINS

"What a delicious color. It's the palest aqua with an almost imperceptible strié."

**NORTHCROFT THROUGH TODD ALEXANDER
ROMANO** | CARNOT IN CANTON; COTTON, POLYESTER
BEST FOR: BERGÈRE

"The pattern is traditional, but in this color it looks young and exciting."

RAOUL TEXTILES | VIZCAYA IN CELERY; OYSTER LINEN

The sleek lines of the slipper chairs prevent its fabric from skewing too traditional. The graphic Greek key motif on both the trim and the pillows add extra contemporary detail.

BRUNSCHWIG & FILS | GAUGUIN LINEN TEXTURE (89588-434) IN AVOCADO; LINEN

Brunschwig & Fils' Gauguin on the sofa counter-balances the strong prints in the room. This solid avocado linen accents the intriguing lines of the sofa, a shape that might disappear beneath a print.

RAOUL TEXTILES | GRANADA IN ROBIN'S EGG; NATURAL LINEN

The cohesiveness of color is what makes this room calm and inviting, says Whittaker, its designer. Medallion print curtains reflect the room's palette and provide another layer of cozy pattern.

CHINA SEAS THROUGH QUADRILLE WALLPAPERS & FABRICS, INC. | NAIROBI IN JUNGLE GREEN ON TINT; LINEN, COTTON

Nothing adds exoticism to a room like an animal print, here on the ottoman in front of the fireplace. While the traditional black and white would have been too fierce in this room, a subtler blue and cream manages to be soothing and dramatic at the same time.

Jaunty prints and clean blue and apple green colorways give a fresh spin on this room by designer **LYNN MORGAN**, who prefers bright, cheery bedrooms to dark cocoons.

VICTORIA HAGAN HOME | EARLY SPRING IN SKY; LINEN

The headboard, bedskirt, and bolster pillow resemble a Matisse cutout and establish blue as this bedroom's dominant color. Morgan finds that the comforting shades of blues and greens create a sense of serenity and warmth.

CHINA SEAS THROUGH QUADRILLE WALLPAPERS & FABRICS, INC. | RIO IN GREEN GRASS ON WHITE; LINEN, COTTON

The dizzy dot print appears twice (once in green on the bench and in blue as bed pillows) and complements the dramatic fabric of the bed nicely. The many prints used as pillows have a common theme: They're all fun, lively, and modern.

PIERRE FREY | SHABBY IN ABSINTHE; LINEN

Morgan needed a strong element to even
out the room. In this case, she upholstered a
chaise lounge in Shabby in Absinthe, a bright
green solid.

FLORAL FANFARE

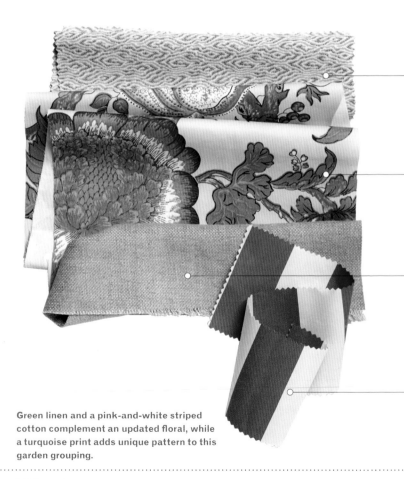

Green linen and a pink-and-white striped cotton complement an updated floral, while a turquoise print adds unique pattern to this garden grouping.

The beauty of creating an indoor garden using floral prints is that these flowers require little attention... and they last forever. **JOE NYE** designed this casual living room based on one vibrant blooming print paired with outdoor furniture for a fun and fresh look.

CURTAIN LINING

"I chose **Vanessa's Folly** to line the striped curtains. Most people get lazy and just do white lining, but a contrasting color has a more finished, couture effect—like you thought about it."

CHAIRS

"**Beauvoir** is the key fabric in the room, the starting-off point. You can pull lots of colors from it. But you have to be careful not to overwhelm the room with it—it's not a timid pattern."

SOFA

"**Brasilia** is a divine color, a wonderful mucky green, and the texture is really cushy. It's comfortable to sit on, even when you're in shorts, so I'd use it in a big way, on a sofa." du**Val**-**Alexander Sofa**.

CURTAINS

"**Striped curtains** are always a winner, and a turquoise lining would really kick off the bright raspberry. With a bold stripe like **Eloi**, I wouldn't do much in the way of trim."

Start Here

**MANUEL CANOVAS THROUGH COWTAN
& TOUT** | BEAUVOIR IN FUCHSIA; COTTON
BEST FOR: CHAIRS

" **These colors are loud and brash—but
in a good way!" Joe Nye says. "It's fun,
but it's busy, so it could get dizzying if
you used a lot of it. The trick is to use
it in a restrained way."**

➕ *Accents* ADD ONE FROM THIS CATEGORY

MANUEL CANOVAS THROUGH COWTAN & TOUT
COTTON CLUB II IN FRAMBOISE; COTTON
BEST FOR: PILLOWS

"It looks like a coarse sailcloth, but it's so soft you want
to put your head on it. I would make two twenty-
two-inch-square pillows with tiny French pleats."

RAOUL TEXTILES | LEOPARD IN OLIVINE; IVORY LINEN
BEST FOR: TABLECLOTH

"I'm crazy for animal prints, so chic! They never
seem to go out of style. I'd use this for a skirted table."

MANUEL CANOVAS THROUGH COWTAN & TOUT
ELOI IN FRAISE; COTTON
BEST FOR: CURTAINS

"For curtains in a sunroom, it's exactly the right look."

Upholstery THEN ADD TWO FROM THIS CATEGORY

BRUNSCHWIG & FILS | VANESSA'S FOLLY COTTON PRINT
IN TURQUOISE; COTTON
BEST FOR: CURTAINS

"I use this all the time to line curtains—it comes in so many colors. I'd do pillows with it, too. Repetition is good—it ties a room together."

MANUEL CANOVAS THROUGH COWTAN & TOUT
INDOCHINE IN CERISE; VISCOSE, COTTON
BEST FOR: OTTOMAN

"This is a strié of cherry red and pink—striés are like solids, but snappier."

MANUEL CANOVAS THROUGH COWTAN & TOUT
BRASILIA IN ANIS; VISCOSE, LINEN
BEST FOR: SOFA

"It's bulletproof. It stands up to hard wear, it's friendly to children, and it's easy to clean."

MANUEL CANOVAS THROUGH COWTAN & TOUT
MAROQUIN IN TILLEUL; COTTON, VISCOSE
BEST FOR: WALLS

"I like to upholster walls, and that's what I'd do with this, for a seamless envelope of the most wonderful green. I'd paint the ceiling the same color."

CARLETON V THROUGH LEE JOFA | RHODODENDRON
IN CREAM; LINEN

Rhododendron, a print made famous by the
legendary Dorothy Draper, is incorporated
because it's bright and happy. Used for both for
the curtains and bed pillows, its massive scale
adds drama and punch to the room.

CARLETON V THROUGH LEE JOFA | ROSSWAY IN
ROSE AND GREEN; COTTON

Two competing large-scale prints would have
overwhelmed this room. Instead, the tranquil
fabric on the quilt complements the more robust
Rhododendron. The reversible bed cover has
Carleton V's Rossway in soft red on one side
and the green on the other.

SEACLOTH THROUGH LEE JOFA | GYPSY BLOOM IN MIDNIGHT; COTTON, LINEN

Floral fabrics don't have to look lifelike. The sofa pillow's bursting blue blooms bestow excitement to the solid sofa, and its bright flowers repeat on the simple wicker chairs.

JANE CHURCHILL THROUGH COWTAN & TOUT FLORIAN PLAIN IN DARK BLUE; COTTON

The sofa's dark blue cotton fabric selection is a practical choice for a home with several young boys. The color hides a multitude of sins, and the sturdy weave holds up well to wear and tear. To Morgan, the room says, "Come on in, everybody's welcome!"

ALAN CAMPBELL THROUGH QUADRILLE WALLPAPERS & FABRICS, INC. | ZIG ZAG (AC 302-18) IN NAVY ON TINT; LINEN, COTTON

Zigzags provide some animated structure against the pillows' soft flowers. Morgan selected navy blues because she knew the boys of the house would appreciate the masculine color.

MIX IT UP

Two overscale prints provide a measured dose of drama, while a shimmery, textured solid serves up some sex appeal. The modern linen sheer keeps everything light.

As president and owner of Dorothy Draper & Co., **CARLETON VARNEY** carries on the design icon's tradition: stylish with unmistakable drama. Color and pattern peacefully coexist in this entrancing living room and each make a powerful impact.

SHEERS
"The vertical line in **Sophie Sheer** is especially useful in a room with low ceilings. The stripe can really add a lot of height."

ACCENT CHAIR
"The dogwood flower in **Malibu** goes so well with the ferns in **Wykeham**. Use **Malibu** on the **Colonnade Armchair** from **Ficks Reed**. The open back keeps things light."

CURTAINS AND ARMCHAIR
"The leaves, the peachy highlight, and the texture—**Wykeham** is magical! Use it for curtains and on the **Lily Chair**. That will tie the window treatment to the rest of the room." **Chair by Kindel.**

SOFA
"I love the silvery reflection of **Siena** so much I'd cover the sofa with it and paint the walls to match." **Varney Sofa from Kindel.**

> ## Start Here

CARLETON V | WYKEHAM IN SPRING GREEN; LINEN
BEST FOR: CURTAINS AND ARMCHAIR

" **There's a charming romance about
this whole combination of ferns and
flowers. The design is like a damask,
but because it's on linen, it's not as
formal, and a bit more feminine.**"

✚ *Upholstery* ADD ONE FROM THIS CATEGORY

CARLETON V | KILLISNOO IN PEAR; COTTON, LINEN
BEST FOR: SOFA, ARMCHAIR, EVERYTHING!

"Stripes are the common denominator in decorating.
If ever in doubt, use a stripe! It goes with everything."

. . . .

TYLER HALL | SUMMER PICNIC IN WHEAT/GRASS;
COTTON, LINEN
BEST FOR: OTTOMAN

"This small chenille check adds dimension to a
room with its coffee and earth-tone lines."

. . . .

CARLETON V | SIENA IN GREEN; COTTON, VISCOSE,
LINEN, SILK
BEST FOR: SOFA

"The texture goes with all the other fabrics in the
room and the shimmery finish looks good both
day and night."

Accents THEN ADD TWO FROM THIS CATEGORY

HINSON & CO. | HINSON SUEDE IN SALMON; MICROFIBER
BEST FOR: ACCENT CHAIR

"A 'pocketbook fabric' like a woman's bag or gloves—just a little bit will be noticed."

CARLETON V | MALIBU IN MANGO; LINEN, COTTON
BEST FOR: PILLOWS AND ACCENT CHAIR

"It's leafy and graphic, which keeps it interesting and fresh."

BASSETT MCNAB COMPANY | JUMPER IN SNAPDRAGON;
RAYON, POLYESTER, NYLON
BEST FOR: PILLOWS

"I love the geometry of a chevron stripe, and this has such luster!"

CARLETON V | SOPHIE SHEER IN LIME; LINEN
BEST FOR: SHEERS

"The silky green stripe gives an otherwise contemporary fabric a layer of tradition."

COLE & SON THROUGH LEE JOFA | COW PARSLEY IN YELLOW; COTTON

In a different room, this bold yellow print by Cole & Son might steal the other fabrics' thunder. When surrounded by fabrics in the same palette, it successfully blends into its surroundings and still manages to maintain its personable spunk.

OSBORNE & LITTLE | CHRYSANTHE IN COLOR 2; LINEN, COTTON

The designer's challenge with a room with fifteen-foot ceilings was to avoid one's eyes from moving upwards. Jeffers managed it by installing roman shades in a similar color to the pale walls, keeping the visual impact at ground level. The fabric on the shades captures all the colors in the sitting room, a trick he typically employs in all his rooms.

ROMO | LEONI IN ICE BLUE; LINEN BLEND

Creamy walls temper the weightiness of a blue rug and upholstered furniture. The headboard, window seat, chairs, and ottoman are covered in a solid linen fabric that feels as casual and comfortable as the rest of the house.

ZOFFANY | MAZE IN BLUE; COTTON, LINEN

While the print selected for the curtains may be a bit busy, when it's paired with solids, the pattern tones down. The curtains help to draw one's eye up and not directly to the darker, heavier elements, balancing the room.

COURAGE WITH COLOR

Jewel-toned fabrics are flush with rich texture: an emerald cotton, a flocked linen flower, a luxurious velvet, and a modern orange pattern.

Such exhilarating color and so many sensual textures, make for a truly contemporary look. New York designer PHILIP GORRIVAN builds this living room inspired by color. In the hands of a master, pinks, greens, blues, and amethysts make for a look not for the faint of heart.

CURTAINS

"I would use Isabelle for curtains. It's a really versatile pattern that works in a city apartment or a country house. The floral pattern isn't overly feminine, and the large scale can make a small room feel larger."

SLIPPER CHAIR

"Although Pacha is a monochromatic fabric, there's a lot going on with texture, and the color is so lively! It's best for tailored pieces."

SOFA

"Veneto is luxurious and grounding, a good foil for breezier fabrics like Isabelle. It also gives a loose-cushion sofa a neat, tailored look." Hamptons Sofa from Intérieurs.

PILLOWS

"Labyrinto has a David Hicks feel—it's sophisticated, glamorous, and very now. As a pillow, the fabric stands on its own, but I could also see adding beaded trim for more detail."

> *Start Here*

HIGHLAND COURT | ISABELLE IN TANGERINE; LINEN
BEST FOR: CURTAINS

" **I wanted to create a flocked fabric that was breezy and elegant. So many are heavy,"** says designer **Philip Gorrivan.** "Isabelle is flocked on linen, with metallic accents, and that keeps it light."

+ *Accents* ADD ONE FROM THIS CATEGORY

HIGHLAND COURT | INTAGLIO IN TANGERINE; RAYON, COTTON
BEST FOR: PILLOWS

"Make pillows with Intaglio. They'd look nice with a knife-edge pleat, a charcoal chocolate brown fringe, or a half-inch grosgrain ribbon surrounding them."

DONGHIA | VICTORIA IN ASTER; RAYON, COTTON
BEST FOR: PILLOWS

"Victoria has a hand-done, embroidered quality. It looks more important as an accent than if you used it to cover an entire sofa."

HIGHLAND COURT | LABYRINTO IN PERSIMMON; RAYON
BEST FOR: SLIPPER CHAIRS

"It has a real punch, a modern feel. The thick weave is ideal for upholstery."

ARCHITEX | MANFRED IN ESPRESSO; COTTON, WOOL
BEST FOR: ARMCHAIR

"Wool épinglé is a lot like velvet—not quite as soft, but equally luxurious and comfortable. Manfred is a little retro, and it can take a room in a younger direction."

HIGHLAND COURT | PACHA IN ABSINTHE; COTTON, RAYON
BEST FOR: SOFA OR CLUB CHAIRS

"Pacha is great on a tailored sofa, or club chairs in a living room or a family room. It could be tufted for a '40s glam look."

HIGHLAND COURT | VENETO IN GRAPHITE; ALPACA VELVET
BEST FOR: SOFA

"I love velvets. What I especially love about Veneto is that it's an alpaca velvet—it's softer, but it's also durable."

BRENTANO FABRICS | MUKHMAL IN MOLASSES;
ACRYLIC, POLYESTER, OLEFIN
BEST FOR: OTTOMAN

"Brown is one of my favorite neutrals. Mukhmal is an acrylic blend that's almost like a textured shag rug. I use it in formal and casual rooms."

NOBILIS | ATLAS (46428) IN CORAL; LINEN

Upholstered in a vibrant coral linen, the sofa pops against the blue walls and rich blue rug. A solid serves as the perfect backdrop for this linen's colorful stripes and dots.

LEE JOFA | RICAMO STRIPE IN SEASIDE; LINEN, COTTON, NYLON

Willey selected the sofa cushion fabric because it reminds him of a striped outdoor awning. Striped cushions and a solid frame make for a quirky combination, but perfectly reflect the laid-back attitude of the island retreat.

LEE JOFA | TWISTER PRINT IN SKY AND TANG; LINEN, COTTON, NYLON

Two throw pillows covered in the aptly named Twister Print seem to vibrate in Technicolor dots against the striped cushions. These two fabrics work well together because both have white backgrounds, which provide some cohesiveness.

PETER DUNHAM TEXTILES | MATTRESS TICKING IN PALE INDIGO; LINEN

Dunham remarks that he likes to "layer all kinds of things until I achieve my own sense of balance." His first layer, replete in Mattress Ticking, is the upholstered walls. The vertical stripes add height, while its subtle gray shade provides a perfect backdrop for the brighter accents in the room.

PETER DUNHAM TEXTILES | KASHMIR PAISLEY IN RED/ BLUE; LINEN

The simplistic Kashmir print in Red and Blue appears here on the bedding. Ample spacing in the pattern keeps the exoticism to its most evasive, and provides an excellent foil to the heavy plush velvet bodypillow.

OUTDOOR INSPIRATION

Outdoor fabrics work well indoors, too,
especially when paired with crisp linen
and luxurious alpaca.

Enjoy the outdoors without even stepping outside. Los Angeles-based designer **ANTONIA HUTT** combines floral acrylics with linens and velvets for a living room that blends the cheeriness of the outdoors with the creature comforts of home.

SOFA

"A bold pattern like Flower Power is really fun on a sofa, and unexpected," says designer Antonia Hutt. Opium Sofa from Christian Liaigre at Holly Hunt.

CURTAINS

"Pizzelle would make beautiful curtains. I'd do a simple triple French pleat and hang them from a wooden pole or a thin silver nickel pole."

PILLOWS

"Prima Alpaca. This is a delicate fabric, not one you'd want to sit on every day, so I'd use it for throw pillows. The luxury of the alpaca against the simplicity of the printed linen would be divine."

CHAIR

"Linara is airy and fresh. The color is like young leaves shooting up on a spring day. Try it on the Soft Breeze chair from David Sutherland and pipe it with something surprising, like hot pink."

Start Here

GALBRAITH & PAUL | FLOWER POWER IN PINK LINEN

BEST FOR: SOFA

" The pattern is primitive in a way, yet modern," says Antonia Hutt. "That metallic in the green gives the print a hint of opulence. I'd pipe it in a contrasting color—if in doubt, go with the green."

Patterns ADD ONE FROM THIS CATEGORY

OLD WORLD WEAVERS THROUGH STARK FABRIC

RAVENNE FLAME STITCH IN AMARANTE; COTTON, SILK, ACRYLIC BLEND

BEST FOR: PILLOWS

"So chic, and fabulous for throw pillows. The shine next to the sofa's matte linen creates a feeling of luxury."

GALBRAITH & PAUL | PIZZELLE IN BABY BLUE; LINEN

BEST FOR: CURTAINS

"I'd do curtains. It's stiff, but I like that look. And I'd also paint my walls the same color turquoise— the curtains become one with the room."

GALBRAITH & PAUL | MOUNTAINS IN KIWI; OYSTER LINEN

BEST FOR: CHAIR

"If you're scared of pattern, this is the fabric for you. A small, dense scale reads more like a solid."

SCHUMACHER | NE PLUS ULTRA IN CADET; COTTON VELVET
BEST FOR: DINING CHAIRS

"Deep colors ground a room but they can also pull things down. You probably wouldn't want this on a sofa. But it's the perfect amount of depth for dining chairs."

. . . .

ROMO | LINARA IN PERIDOT; COTTON, LINEN
BEST FOR: CHAIR

"I'm never afraid to use bright colors in upholstery. They can lift a room's spirits. Create what makes you happy and forget other people's rules."

. . . .

SANDRA JORDAN | PRIMA ALPACA IN PARCELA; ALPACA
BEST FOR: SOFA

"If I could, I'd cover everything in my house in Prima Alpaca. It's the most gorgeous and luxurious fabric I've ever seen. Even the color is luxurious."

. . . .

LELIEVRE THROUGH STARK FABRIC | LE JAZZ IN CORAIL; POLYESTER
BEST FOR:

"I'd put Le Jazz on furniture that gets a lot of sun. The more intense the color, the greater the chance of fading, but this is polyester—it won't fade."

Everything about this **BARCLAY BUTERA-designed** bathroom is evocative of the outdoors, especially the green and brown color scheme and the nature motif prints. It's a look that Butera christened "Asian beach chic."

BARCLAY BUTERA HOME | ABSTRACT IN CREAM AND BROWN; COTTON SLUB DUCK

In this Zen bathroom, things take a playful turn with the bench's bamboo print, a retro interpretation of the traditional Asian motif. The crisscross bamboo lends a strong diagonal dimension to the fabric arrangement.

KRAVET | GRACE IN PERIDOT; VISCOSE, POLYESTER, SILK

Butera chose the central pillow's fabric because it reminded him of 1960s Palm Beach. While the print is loose, the brown background keeps things grounded. Helping to center the scheme are the palm frond pillows that tie together the two prints.

For clients in **Nantucket**, T. KELLER DONOVAN conceives a living room steeped in shades of nautical blue. Were it not for the walls and ceiling, you might think you were out at sea.

ROMO | LINARA IN ELECTRIC BLUE; COTTON, LINEN

Throughout the house, Donovan used a family friendly cotton/linen blend that's practical for sticky little hands. Its classic shade of blue appropriate for a seaside town works well with the spare lines of the wicker furniture, and the natural wicker helps to give the crisp blue cushions further prominence.

PETER FASANO, LTD. | CAMP LEAVES; LINEN

Camp Leaves features a stylized print that's a botanical with a twist. Its blue and tan shades help keep the atmosphere of the room calming, even when surrounded by snappy prints, an overscale plaid rug, and a painted convex mirror.

PETER FASANO, LTD. | DOTTY; LINEN

A dotted print flanks French doors and spruces
up the window shades. Its neutral background
blends seamlessly with the creamy white falls,
and the pattern seems to create movement—like
blue dots falling from the sky.

FRENCH CONNECTION

A faded green stripe and a soft blue linen
in supporting colors mix well, while a strong
green geometric pattern provides a delightful
surprise.

A room shouldn't be too perfect—it should always hold a surprise or two. Here's Sister Parish protégée **LIBBY CAMERON'S** ideal mix of traditional and cozy. This small sitting room, inspired by the soft florals and vivid colors, help to achieve a bright and cheery space with some vibrant prints.

ARMCHAIR

"A pair of upholstered chairs in **Rolling Meadow** will anchor the room. I love it with the shape and simplicity of the **Mecox Library Chair** from **Mecox Gardens.**"

CURTAINS

"**Patmos Stripe** will add height to the room. The curtains should be quite simple and hang from poles and rings with decorative finials."

SOFA

"**Lido** is soft yet sturdy. Great for a sofa, since it won't wrinkle too much or feel fragile to sit on." **2016-72 Sofa** from **O. Henry House** through **John Rosselli & Associates.**

BENCH

"If you use too much **Tuckerman**, it will compete with the hydrangea fabric. Use just a bit on the **Brighton Bench,** from **John Rosselli & Associates,** to highlight the green."

> *Start Here*

WAVERLY | ROLLING MEADOW IN CHAMBRAY;
LINEN, RAYON
BEST FOR: PAIR OF CHAIRS

" It's a printed linen with an old-fashioned
feel, but in a modern palette. The vibrant
chartreuse makes the fabric feel fresh
and young. Pull out the creams, greens,
and taupes with small-patterned fabrics."

+ *Accents* ADD ONE FROM THIS CATEGORY

TRAVERS THROUGH ZIMMER + ROHDE | OAKLEAVES
IN BLUE; LINEN
BEST FOR: PILLOWS

"This graphic floral is abstract and perfect for pull-
ing the blue out of Rolling Meadow."

. . . .

**SISTER PARISH DESIGN THROUGH JOHN ROSSELLI &
ASSOCIATES, LTD.** | TUCKERMAN IN GREEN; COTTON TWILL
BEST FOR: BENCH

"It's visually strong and adds a shot of energy without being too much."

. . . .

KATHRYN M. IRELAND | TONAL TICKING IN GREEN; HEMP
BEST FOR: LAMPSHADES

"Playful and quiet at the same time, with enough
pattern to keep things interesting."

Anchors THEN ADD TWO FROM THIS CATEGORY

CAROLINA IRVING TEXTURES | PATMOS STRIPE IN
PARSLEY; HEMP
BEST FOR: CURTAINS

"The colors are soothing, and the design won't
challenge the other fabrics."

. . . .

JANE SHELTON | LADDER STRIPE IN BROWN; COTTON
BEST FOR: PULL-UP CHAIR

"It has more character than most stripes—it reminds
me of seersucker."

. . . .

CLARENCE HOUSE | LIDO IN OFF-WHITE; VISCOSE, LINEN
BEST FOR: SOFA

"I love the feel of a heavy linen. The texture holds
its own in a room."

. . . .

**SISTER PARISH DESIGN THROUGH JOHN ROSSELLI
& ASSOCIATES, LTD.** | LOGAN IN GREEN; COTTON
BEST FOR: ARMCHAIR

"A simple, soft, cottony chenille in a great color.
Over time, it will only get softer."

RAOUL TEXTILES | PALOMA IN DELFT; OYSTER LINEN
An antique spool bed hosts a riot of prints in
shades of bright blue and white. The ethnic and
geometric prints lend a bold beachy look.

RAOUL TEXTILES | ANANAS IN CIEL; OYSTER LINEN
The outermost throw pillows, covered in Tea Leaf,
closely resemble the seat cushions's Paloma. They
don't clash due to their parallel color palettes.

RAOUL TEXTILES | SCROLL PAISLEY IN MAJOLICA;
OYSTER LINEN
The tight pattern of Scroll Paisley reads as a
solid from afar, while the center pillow with its
simple blue stripe provides a splash of white.
This bold grouping works because the small
patters are concentrated in a small footprint.

LULU DK | WELLINGTON IN CHOCOLATE; LINEN, VISCOSE
Mindful of the green and brown colorway, Willey begins by upholstering the twin headboards in a crosshatch print, serving as a masculine foil for the more feminine butterflies and ikat.

CHINA SEAS THROUGH QUADRILLE WALLPAPERS & FABRICS, INC. | ISLAND IKAT (6460-09) IN PALM GREEN ON WHITE; LINEN
Roman shades in a verdant green and white ikat print present a splash of color and pattern against a neutral grasscloth wallpaper. It also appears on bed pillows. Selecting prints from the same woodsy colors allows Willey to have a larger selection of prints and patterns.

MURIEL BRANDOLINI THROUGH HOLLAND & SHERRY
WHITE NO. 5; INDIAN COTTON
A whimsical cotton butterfly duvet cover is the wild card print in the room, but it stays within the room's theme and muted colorway. Brown butterflies complement the headboard and rug.

CHAPTER

3

THE FRESH
EXOTICS

GLOBETROTTING PRINTS

An ikat, an Indian paisley, and a Persian print have equal billing, while the star print is the modern addition to the group.

Don't limit yourself to just one culture's exotic fabrics. Mix and match to create a room like one of **PETER DUNHAM'S** dazzling interiors, which he describes as "half Jackie Kennedy goes to Jaipur and half Brigitte Bardot 1960s South of France." Would you expect anything less from a globe-hopping British designer?

SOFA

"Ikat is great for this sofa. The red isn't too intense, and the pattern breaks up the large piece of upholstery, giving it some sexiness." **Grant Sofa from Hollywood at Home.**

CURTAINS

"The scale of Samarkand is so big and has such integrity. Through the curtain fold, you'll get glimpses of the paisley—so romantic."

CHAIR

"Kashmir Paisley has the geometric punch of David Hicks fabric from the '60s. It lightens the chair and also gives it a timeless look." **Barrymore Chair from Hollywood at Home.**

OTTOMAN

"Starburst adds sparkle and takes some seriousness out of the room." **Garner Ottoman from Hollywood at Home.**

▶ *Start Here*

PETER DUNHAM TEXTILES | SAMARKAND IN BLUE/RED; LINEN
BEST FOR: CURTAINS OR WALLS

" **A friend had a nineteenth-century
Persian tablecloth he bought in Tangiers.
I always loved it, so I adapted it. Both men
and women feel comfortable with ethnic
prints. It's bold, but easy to live with.**"

✚ *Upholstery* ADD ONE FROM THIS CATEGORY

KATHRYN M. IRELAND | WOVEN IN RED; LINEN
BEST FOR: SOFA

"A thick linen that's sink-in comfortable. The
tweedy weave has depth, and it breaks up the red
so it's not overpowering."

. . . .

JASPER THROUGH MICHAEL S. SMITH | GAVLE IN
BLUE; LINEN
BEST FOR: SOFA OR ARMCHAIR

"It's sumptuous but understated, and I love the color.
The uneven weave adds great texture to the room."

. . . .

PETER DUNHAM TEXTILES | IKAT IN POMEGRANATE; LINEN
BEST FOR: SOFA OR CURTAINS

"Easy to layer with other fabrics, and it can be
used in a modern or traditional setting."

Accents THEN ADD TWO FROM THIS CATEGORY

PETER DUNHAM TEXTILES | STARBURST IN EAST; LINEN
BEST FOR: OTTOMAN

"This is a happy fabric. It puts a smile on my face."

CAROLINA IRVING TEXTILES | PATMOS STRIPE IN
POMPEII; HEMP
BEST FOR: PILLOWS

"It's breezy but complex. I love the vintage look."

JED JOHNSON HOME | MEDALLION IN IMPERIAL;
COTTON, LINEN
BEST FOR: ACCENT CHAIR

"The embroidery makes it super luxe, but the design is simple. I wish I had designed it myself!"

PETER DUNHAM TEXTILES | KASHMIR PAISLEY IN RED/
BLUE; LINEN
BEST FOR: ARMCHAIR

"I call it a 'go-everywhere' print, because it mixes with almost anything."

MADELINE WEINRIB | DASHWOOD; SILK, COTTON
An ikat print on the bench cushion serves up a
burst of color and pattern in an otherwise muted
space. The fabric contrasts interestingly with the
antique bench and the aged heraldic crest.

MADELINE WEINRIB | MU IN BROWN; SILK, COTTON
A set of strié polka dot pillows provides yet another
exotic layer. When combining prints and fabrics,
Kincaid says she puts them all down on the floor
and squints her eyes and looks at them to make
sure her eyes don't jump around too much.

KRAVET | NATCHEZ IN SPICE; RAYON, COTTON

Kyser designed the library for her husband, who is a big fan of Graham Green. Because she was going for a vintage look, Kyser decided to upholster the armchairs in an ikat print that provides a dash of mystery and exoticism.

LIBECO-LAGAE | P533 IN ARABICA; BELGIAN LINEN

The sofa in a solid Belgian linen acts as a blank canvas for a collection of pillows representing a spectrum of cultures: antique silk ikats and nineteenth-century Thai fabric. The solid linen hides any shedding fur from the family's black Labs.

C&C MILANO THROUGH HOLLAND & SHERRY
PIENZA RAFANO IN BLUE NATURAL; LINEN

The designer wanted a great deal of rich overlapping pattern, so she used this small graphic print on an armchair throw pillow. The abundant layering of prints establishes a sense of coziness and warmth.

EAST MEETS WEST

This elegant and eclectic collection includes
stripes and prints as well as bold solids;
textures create layers where none is expected.

"When I was growing up, we never used our living room," says designer **BARCLAY BUTERA**. Here he imagines a living room you'd never ever leave. The L.A.-based designer collects fabrics partially inspired by striking colors and patterns from the Orient. "It's about beautiful patterns you can layer."

CURTAINS
"Carrey is light and bright. I see it for curtains—pinch-pleated on iron rings and hung from a burnished bamboo rod."

PILLOWS
"I like blending styles—paisley, stripes, the Chinese emblems on Realm. The flocked medallion has a balance and symmetry that is great for pillows."

WING CHAIR
"Run Ennobled vertically up my Grant Wing Chair. The chocolate and blood orange stripes play with the lines of the curvy arms." Chair from Barclay Butera Home.

SOFA
"Westwood really lightens a room. With its tufting and brass nailheads, the Manchester Sofa makes the fabric look crisp." Sofa from Barclay Butera Home.

> *Start Here*

BARCLAY BUTERA THROUGH KRAVET
CARREY IN BRICK; LINEN, SILK
BEST FOR: CURTAINS

" **This was inspired by a great paisley scarf. We printed it on an ecru background to get a softer color, a muted Chinese red. It's playful, not serious.**"

+ *Accents* ADD ONE FROM THIS CATEGORY

BARCLAY BUTERA THROUGH KRAVET | REALM IN CHINESE RED; LINEN, COTTON
BEST FOR: PILLOWS, UPHOLSTERY DETAIL

"It's a novelty, a little '70s, but updated. Center it on top of a small ottoman."

. . . .

SCHUMACHER | VAUGHAN CHENILLE IN PERSIMMON; ACRYLIC, POLYESTER, COTTON
BEST FOR: PILLOWS

"This is another surprise—a zigzag chenille. Small touches of strong patterns are a must."

. . . .

KRAVET | SILK SKIN IN GARNET; LINEN, SILK, RAYON
BEST FOR: MORE PILLOWS

"I love animal prints as an accent. The slight metallic sheen gives the perfect dose of glamour."

Upholstery THEN ADD TWO FROM THIS CATEGORY

BARCLAY BUTERA THROUGH KRAVET | ENNOBLED IN
LANTERN RED; VISCOSE, COTTON
BEST FOR: WING CHAIR

"The cut velvet is soft, the texture so rich. Put it on a chair for a very cozy place to sit."

BARCLAY BUTERA HOME | ABSOLUTE IN TOMATO;
LEATHER
BEST FOR: OTTOMAN

"This type of polished leather works best on smaller pieces. The color just pops!"

RALPH LAUREN HOME | WESTWOOD IN RATTAN; RAYON,
NYLON, POLYESTER
BEST FOR: SOFA

"Look for a neutral with a lot of texture for the dominant fabric in a room."

RALPH LAUREN HOME | NIGEL IN HARVEST; MOHAIR
BEST FOR: SOFA

"This mohair is rich. It has depth. Wouldn't it look great on a big comfy sofa?"

SANDERSON THROUGH ZOFFANY | PINSTRIPE; LINEN BLEND

Sanderson's Pinstripe, pops from its place uphol-stered on the study's walls. While the dark brown may overwhelm in a room with less light, the sheer curtains and large white mantle serve as an excellent foil to the walls.

QUADRILLE WALLPAPERS & FABRICS, INC. NOTTINGHAM IN TAN; VISCOSE, ACRYLIC

A velvet paisley used for both the sofa and desk chair reflects the masculine feel of the room, while the airy fabric helps to cast light into the dark brown room. Nailhead trim on the sofa provides a node to the man of the house.

SCALAMANDRÉ | PING IN COFFEE; LINEN

The whimsical chinoiserie print on the curtains helps add to the lighthearted nature of the room. Born as Western interpretations of fanciful Asian scenes, chinoiserie prints are traditionally lively.

This relaxed **Los Angeles** family room, designed by **MARY MCDONALD**, presents a riddle: Did the Asian accessories inspire the choice of fabrics, or was it the other way around?

COWTAN & TOUT | RAPHAELLO (10817-03) IN DELFT; LINEN, COTTON

The table skirt's print takes on additional Oriental flair when placed beneath the Chinese export vases. The blue and white colorway, shown here in a youthful, bright fabric, is often seen in antique Asian porcelain.

RAOUL TEXTILES | OCEAN FLOWERS (420N84) IN PIMENTO; NATURAL LINEN

An exotic floral on the sofas adds a breezy vibe to this sunny room. The print's pattern leaves much of the cream background visible, which helps to brighten the space. Asian garden stools, books, and the carved boxes on the ottoman further extend the red palette into the room's center.

PASSAGE TO INDIA

A delicate floral mixes seamlessly with a
large-scale print, while a **Greek** key velvet and a
textured cotton ensure the mix stays modern.

Afraid to dip your toe into a sea of exotic pattern? Try layers of texture and patterns with a hint of global sophistication. **KATIE RIDDER** creates rooms that meld influences from around the world. For this study inspired by Les Indiennes, she proposes hand-blocked cottons based on traditional Indian designs.

CURTAINS

"I like the natural imperfections of Elise. It has a warm, handmade feeling that I love. You can use it anywhere, but I like it best for simple curtains."

PILLOWS

"I use Philip for accent pillows. The big scale of that swirly pattern is perfect—it's a nice shift from the rest of the smaller-scale fabrics."

CHAIR

"Min has a small repeat that's lovely on a wood-framed chair like this Gillows Spoonbill Chair from Soane. What a showstopping combination."

SOFA

"This is a great sofa fabric for people who don't want to commit to a pattern. Boutis is a solid, but it has a subtle graphic texture that keeps it interesting. It's fabulous on the Elaine Sofa from Classic Sofa."

▶ *Start Here*

LES INDIENNES | ELISE IN OLIVE; COTTON
BEST FOR: CURTAINS

" I like the contrast of Elise with these dressier fabrics," says Katie Ridder. "It's a casual cotton, and it blends everything in a very confident way."

✚ *Accents* ADD ONE FROM THIS CATEGORY

RAOUL TEXTILES | PHILIP IN CARDAMON; NATURAL LINEN
BEST FOR: PILLOWS

"Philip is perfect for big twenty-inch-square accent pillows," says Ridder. "The dark ground of this natural linen also looks so pretty in a room with upholstered white walls."

. . . .

LES INDIENNES | LA REINE IN OLIVE; COTTON
BEST FOR: PILLOWS

"Les Indiennes fabrics go anywhere. The cottons will make a great shower curtain, or Roman shades in the kitchen, and pillows in the living room."

. . . .

NEISHA CROSLAND THROUGH STARK FABRIC
BERRY FLOWER IN LEMON CURD; COTTON
BEST FOR: CHAIRS

"I'd use it to upholster a pair of petite chairs and then put them on either side of a sofa."

Upholstery THEN ADD TWO FROM THIS CATEGORY

JENNIFER ROBBINS TEXTILES | MIN IN MER WITH
PLATINUM; SILK, RAYON
BEST FOR: CHAIR

"The embroidered silk gives Min a Shanghai feel.
It's a unique pattern that would be so pretty on a
chair—especially a framed chair."

. . . .

SCALAMANDRÉ | OASIS IN IVORY, BLUE, AND YELLOW;
LINEN, POLYESTER
BEST FOR: CHAIR

"The linen/polyester print Oasis has a more vertical pattern. I'd upholster a seat and seat-back in it,
then cover the rest of the chair in a watery blue."

. . . .

DEDAR | BOUTIS IN EBANO; COTTON, NYLON
BEST FOR: SOFA

"Boutis can be dressy. I've used it as a sofa fabric,
and welted it with a contrasting color. In this
case, I'd use a yellowy green. Chartreuse would
be gorgeous."

. . . .

HOLLAND & SHERRY | CHAMONIX IN WHITE; WOOL
BEST FOR: WALLS

"Upholster walls in Chamonix and then accentuate
the architecture by trimming it with nailheads."

In a house more **Americana** than exotic,
TOM STRINGER sprinkles ethnic prints on
traditional fabrics to add a dash of glamour.

RAOUL TEXTILES | PASHA IN DELFT; OYSTER LINEN
A sturdy white linen print inspired by India appears
as throw pillows on both sofas. Its subtle blue and
white pattern is soft enough to play backup to the
sofa's bolder prints.

RAOUL TEXTILES | SCROLL PAISLEY IN MAJOLICA;
OYSTER LINEN
There's "a fine line between looking simple and
looking slapped together," says designer Stringer.
Raoul Textiles' Scroll Paisley appears on both the
throw pillows and window shades and ties the
room together in a tailored fashion.

LULU DK | CHANT REVERSE IN ROYAL BLUE; LINEN, COTTON
Graphic prints work well with exotics. Its contemporary fabric and bright palette helps to counteract the
stronger blues in the rest of the room.

RAOUL TEXTILES | LIMOGES IN CIEL; OYSTER LINEN
The circular print of the two end cushions skews
more traditional than ethnic, and provides excellent contrast to the sofa.

CARLETON V | WALLIS TICKING IN GRASS; COTTON

Roberts opts for classic cotton ticking on the banquette—a good spot for naps. While the cushions are upholstered in a straight vertical fashion, the pillows are mitered in two different patterns. Roberts uses the same ticking as trim for the window shades, which look finished, not fussy.

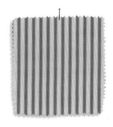

BRUNSCHWIG & FILS | BOTTICELLI IN LICHEN; COTTON, VELVET

Although velvet seems an unlikely choice for this casual sunroom, its unexpected nature makes it more interesting. The luxuriousness of Botticelli just begs one to sit down and linger over a meal or a game of cards.

UNDERSTATED EXOTICS

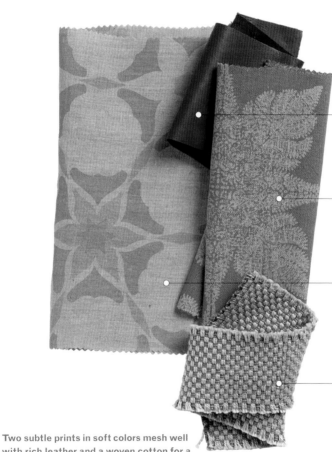

Two subtle prints in soft colors mesh well
with rich leather and a woven cotton for a
refreshing look with sophisticated appeal.

Designer **MADELINE STUART'S** low-key exotic prints won't overwhelm a room. She describes her style as "uncluttered and unpretentious." To that we add warm, stylish, and timeless, too. Her family room is filled with great spots for conversation, comfortable upholstery, and overflowing bookshelves.

OTTOMAN

"Hoof It provides depth and richness to the color scheme, and it wears beautifully."
Ottoman from Madeline Stuart Collection.

PILLOWS

"Use Cinde for pillows on the sofa. It's so cozy and soft. I always under-fill my pillows and use all down so they're more like bed pillows."

LOUNGE CHAIRS

"I would put Stellar on a pair of my O'Hara Lounge Chairs. The simple lines would show off the elegant geometry of the pattern."
Chair from Madeline Stuart Collection.

SOFA

"Thebes is terribly sturdy, and the texture will hide dirt that is inevitably found in a family room. It looks especially good on the Burlingame Sofa, finished with nailheads along the base."

Start Here

VANDERHURD | STELLAR 4 IN GREY AND CHARTREUSE; NATURAL LINEN
BEST FOR: PAIR OF LOUNGE CHAIRS

" **The colors are a bit unusual—nothing particularly trendy, but still fresh. And I like how the print isn't overly active. Cover a pair of comfortable lounge chairs—and don't forget the nailheads.**"

Accents ADD ONE FROM THIS CATEGORY

VANDERHURD | DAISY CHAIN 17 IN SILVER AND CHARTREUSE; CHANDERI
BEST FOR: SHEERS
"Sunlight filtered through will give the room a sense of tranquility you can't get from lined curtains."

JOHN ROBSHAW | CINDE IN MONSOON; LINEN, COTTON
BEST FOR: PILLOWS
"This is such a lovely fabric. The delicacy of the pattern is exquisite."

VANDERHURD | FLOWER STENCIL 5 IN CHARTREUSE; NATURAL LINEN
BEST FOR: CURTAINS OR PILLOWS
"The taupey ground softens the acid yellow, so it's a surprisingly quiet yet forceful presence in the room."

Upholstery THEN ADD TWO FROM THIS CATEGORY

CHAPAS TEXTILES | THEBES IN CACTUS; COTTON
BEST FOR: SOFA

"A favorite of mine for the beauty of the materials and artisanal quality. It's completely handwoven!"

....

CLAREMONT | SERGE ANTIQUE IN COLOR 92; RAYON, COTTON
BEST FOR: SIDE CHAIR

"It may look plain, but it's not. There's texture and depth in the weave. And the color! You can see it from across a crowded room."

....

JERRY PAIR LEATHER | HOOF IT IN COGNAC; LEATHER
BEST FOR: OTTOMAN

"This is a gorgeous leather. The color reminds me of Georgia clay—not quite red, not quite brown."

....

GEORGE SPENCER DESIGNS THROUGH CLAREMONT
UNO IN NATURAL; LINEN
BEST FOR: SOFA

"A foil for all those fabulous pillow fabrics because it acts as a neutral canvas without being dullsville."

JASPER THROUGH MICHAEL S. SMITH | REMY 1515 IN BLUE; HEMP

When paired with restrained fabrics, the sofa, with its exotic batik print, stands out as the room's focus. Its bold fabric choice doesn't dominate because it doesn't break with the color palette of the living room and adjacent dining room.

TRAVERS THROUGH ZIMMER + ROHDE | RENISHAW (400143) IN MELON; VISCOSE, LINEN

The designers set out to create harmony with balance. To do so, they selected a coral solid for the sofa's throw pillows, picking up on the walls of the dining room (not pictured).

JASPER THROUGH MICHAEL S. SMITH | KASHMIR IN SAFFRON; HEMP

While exotic flourishes fill the bedroom, what keeps it soft and peaceful is each print's similar, muted tones. The walls and curtains are Kashmir, a classic paisley. Because pattern flourishes in the room, no single fabric manages to take the upper hand.

JASPER THROUGH MICHAEL S. SMITH | JAMMU IN SAFFRON; LINEN

Kincaid is a fan of Indian-style prints, and she likes to pick fabrics with character, something which describes the half canopies and bedskirts. The quilted throws introduce yet another exotic pattern. Kincaid believes that the union of these various prints proves successful because they create such visual interest.

VOYAGE AROUND THE WORLD

An untraditional tree of life print pairs nicely
with graphic pattern and a glamorous metallic
linen, resulting in a wonderful tour de force.

Some exotics are so easy to work with that you can use them almost anywhere. A perfect example is **CELERIE KEMBLE'S** eponymous fabric collection. Here, she designs a fashionable living room that is both chic and modern. She says, "I wasn't thinking couture as much as ready-to-wear. I didn't want designs that were so exotic they weren't useful in a thousand different ways."

SLIPPER CHAIR

"I love the beaded fretwork of Bleecker. It looks great against the tapered, squarish frame of the Genna chair from my own line for Laneventure."

SOFA

"After seeing a hundred too many solid sofas, I've been hankering for one in a modern floral like Hot House Flowers." 5701-03 Sofa by Celerie for Laneventure.

OTTOMAN

"I like Betwixt on my playfully shaped Gigi ottoman. It creates a splash of pattern down low." Ottoman by Celerie for Laneventure.

CHAIR

"Glimmer is a glamorous silver. It works with the Regent Chair because both are so flirty!" Regent chair by Jonathan Adler.

> *Start Here*

SCHUMACHER | HOT HOUSE FLOWERS IN
MINERAL; LINEN
BEST FOR: SOFA

" **It's a traditional tree of life pattern in idea
only. I made it outlandish with imaginary
flowers and colors that are vibrant and
versatile—slate, pale blue, chalky white,
and a natural, hempy linen."**

+ *Accents* ADD ONE FROM THIS CATEGORY

MADELINE WEINRIB | DAPHNE IN HAZELNUT; SILK, COTTON
BEST FOR: PILLOWS

"I have a long-standing ikat addiction! I can't resist
the scale and the colors like this one in taupe-pink
and navy."

SCHUMACHER | BETWIXT IN CHARCOAL/ECRU; COTTON
BEST FOR: OTTOMAN

"There's something so chipper about the pattern.
You can feel the texture with your eyes."

KRAVET | 8590 IN COLOR 1; POLYACRYLIC BLEND
BEST FOR: UNLINED CURTAINS

"As a sheer, it softens the cold, hard glass of big
windows...gives a bit of privacy without blocking
out the light."

Upholstery THEN ADD TWO FROM THIS CATEGORY

SCHUMACHER | BLEECKER IN TWILIGHT; LINEN
BEST FOR: SLIPPER CHAIR

"I love its energy! It channels the personality of a polka dot with the graphic zip of a geometric."

SCHUMACHER | BAGAN IN BISCUIT; LINEN, SILK
BEST FOR: CURTAINS

"Light as silk but not glossy, fussy, or fancy. A wide stripe with a blurry edge: It's very simple and graceful."

VALTEKZ | MORAY IN POMEGRANATE; PVC, COTTON
BEST FOR: WALLS

"It's mod, it's sexy, it's indestructible. It has all the heft and importance of leather, but animal friendly!"

SCHUMACHER | GLIMMER IN MINERAL; ACRYLIC,
COTTON BLEND
BEST FOR: CHAIR

"A linen with the look and feel of silk velvet— and it's the color of a cloud's silver lining."

DONGHIA | LANAI IN BLUE; ACRYLIC

The designers chose blue upholstery for the house because when you've been on the beach in the bright sun all day, it's very restful to encounter cooler colors. All of the home's fabrics are indoor-outdoor fabric for easy maintenance.

DONGHIA | OAHU IN LIGHT BLUE/BLUE; ACRYLIC

The island print on the throw pillows, aptly named Oahu, are not only appropriate for the house's locale, but contemporary enough to blend in with the house's clean, modern lines. The rattan furniture completes the look.

RALPH LAUREN HOME | COASTAL STRIPE IN YELLOW AND WHITE; COTTON

Working with a blue, yellow, and white color palette, Stringer upholstered the headboard of a four-poster bed with this sunny stripe. Its classic nature and the whitewashed walls and ceiling make this room quintessentially American.

RAOUL TEXTILES | CHUNARI IN BLUE WILLOW; NATURAL LINEN

Exotic prints might surprise in a room like this, but these versatile prints blend flawlessly with their surroundings. Because of the room's pale walls, Stringer knew that the upholstery of these benches and their unique shape would pop.

RAOUL TEXTILES | SARI IN SAFFRON; OYSTER LINEN

Stringer wanted throw pillows that would add a graphic element, so he used a breezy print that perfectly captures the room's entire color palette. Also pictured: Raoul Textiles' Scroll Paisley in Majolica.

FABRIC SWATCHES

FLOWERS AND FOLIAGE

BRUNSCHWIG & FILS
VERRIERES GLAZED CHINTZ IN
BLUE/WHITE (75922-04); COTTON
page 18

LEE JOFA
ALTHEA LINEN PRINT IN
CITRON (2000162-23); LINEN
page 18

KOPLAVITCH & ZIMMER
FUSCARI IN TRUFFLE/CREAM;
COTTON, SILK
page 19

BENNISON
DRAGON FLOWER IN ORIGINAL ON
BEIGE; LINEN, COTTON, POLYAMIDE
page 21

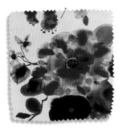

**RUBELLI THROUGH
BERGAMO FABRICS**
CAP D'ANTIBES IN MULTICOLOUR;
LINEN | page 21

COWTAN & TOUT
ORIANA IN ROSE, BLUE,
WHITE; COTTON
page 26

OSBORNE & LITTLE
COPELAND IN COLOR 03; LINEN,
COTTON, VISCOSE
page 26

**ROSE CUMMING THROUGH
DESSIN FOURNIR**
DELPHINIUM IN WHITE; COTTON
page 27

**ISAAC MIZRAHI THROUGH
S. HARRIS FABRICS**
MEGA CHINTZ IN CITRUS; LINEN
page 27

FLOWERS AND FOLIAGE

CLARENCE HOUSE
DAHLIA IN MULTI; LINEN
page 32

**C&C MILANO THROUGH
HOLLAND & SHERRY**
PIENZA CARCIOFINO IN WHITE
NATURAL; LINEN | page 35

**NINA CAMPBELL THROUGH
OSBORNE & LITTLE**
DELPHINE IN COLOR 01; LINEN
page 38

**CHINA SEAS THROUGH
QUADRILLE WALLPAPERS
& FABRICS, INC.**
HAWTHORNE 3015-05 IN SKY ON
TAN; LINEN | page 40

**ANNIE SELKE
HOME THROUGH CALICO
CORNERS**
SCRAMBLE IN CHOCOLATE; LINEN,
RAYON | page 43

COWTAN & TOUT
MINTON IN AQUA; VISCOSE,
COTTON, LINEN
page 47

**G P & J BAKER
THROUGH LEE JOFA**
J0571-3 IN BLUE/AQUA; SILK
page 48

RAOUL TEXTILES
TEALEAF IN DELFT;
OYSTER LINEN
page 50

TYLERGRAPHIC
PAISLEY IN PINK; LINEN
page 54

FABRIC SWATCHES

FLOWERS AND FOLIAGE

COLEFAX AND FOWLER THROUGH COWTAN & TOUT
CALDBECK IN BLUE; LINEN
page 56

GREY WATKINS THROUGH STARK FABRIC
AURORA BELLA IN TAN; LINEN
page 59

KATHRYN M. IRELAND
FLORAL BATIK IN PINK WITH GREEN; HEMP LINEN
page 62

KATHRYN M. IRELAND
IKAT IN GREEN; HEMP LINEN
page 63

KATHRYN M. IRELAND
DIAMOND BATIK IN RED; HEMP LINEN
page 63

LEE JOFA
MADELINE WEAVE IN RASPBERRY; COTTON, VISCOSE
page 63

JASPER THROUGH MICHAEL S. SMITH
TREE OF LIFE IN SAGE; HEMP
page 75

SCHUMACHER
BEATRICE BOUQUET IN MINERAL; LINEN, POLYAMIDE
page 78

BRAQUENIE THROUGH PIERRE FREY
LE GRAND GENOIS RAYURE 4 CHEMINS IN MULTICOLORE; COTTON | page 86

FABRIC SWATCHES

FLOWERS AND FOLIAGE

**COLEFAX AND FOWLER
THROUGH COWTAN & TOUT**
FLORAL TOILE IN BLUE; LINEN,
COTTON | page 90

LEE JOFA
QUEEN JULIE IN BLACK;
WOOL, COTTON
page 94

OLD WORLD WEAVERS
GARIBALDI IN
ADRIATICA; ACRYLIC
page 96

ROBERT ALLEN
NURTURE IN TIDAL;
VISCOSE BLEND
page 102

LEE JOFA
NYMPHEUS PRINT IN
NATURAL; LINEN
page 110

**QUADRILLE WALLPAPERS
& FABRICS, INC.**
SAN MICHELE IN ROSSO ON
BEIGE; LINEN | page 120

**GROUNDWORKS
THROUGH LEE JOFA**
DEJI PRINT IN CARNIVAL; COTTON
page 120

**JANE CHURCHILL
THROUGH COWTAN & TOUT**
ROSAMUND IN GREEN; COTTON,
VISCOSE, LINEN, NYLON | page 121

**CHINA SEAS THROUGH
QUADRILLE WALLPAPERS
& FABRICS, INC.**
LYSETTE REVERSE 4100-11 IN
MAGENTA ON TAN; LINEN | page 122

FABRIC SWATCHES

FLOWERS AND FOLIAGE

**CHINA SEAS THROUGH
QUADRILLE WALLPAPERS
& FABRICS, INC.**
LYSETTE REVERSE 4100-03 IN PALM
GREEN ON TAN; LINEN | page 122

PINE CONE HILL
LONGPOINT IN CITRUS;
COTTON TWILL
page 128

PINE CONE HILL
STAR CREWEL IN LEAF; COTTON
WITH WOOL EMBROIDERY
page 128

PINE CONE HILL
UMA IN INDIGO; COTTON
page 129

BRUNSCHWIG & FILS
MONTBARD LINEN AND COTTON
PRINT IN LEMON; LINEN
page 133

T4 FABRICS
LARGE PANSY IN DANUBE
BLUE; LINEN
page 136

VICTORIA HAGAN HOME
EARLY SPRING IN SKY; LINEN
page 140

**MANUEL CANOVAS
THROUGH COWTAN & TOUT**
BEAUVOIR IN FUCHSIA; COTTON
page 144

**CARLETON V
THROUGH LEE JOFA**
RHODODENDRON IN CREAM; LINEN
page 147

228 | FABRIC INDEX

FABRIC SWATCHES

FLOWERS AND FOLIAGE

**CARLETON V
THROUGH LEE JOFA**
ROSSWAY IN ROSE & GREEN;
COTTON | page 147

**SEACLOTH
THROUGH LEE JOFA**
GYPSY BLOOM IN MIDNIGHT;
COTTON, LINEN | page 148

CARLETON V
WYKEHAM IN SPRING
GREEN; LINEN
page 152

**COLE & SON
THROUGH LEE JOFA**
COW PARSLEY IN YELLOW; COTTON
page 154

OSBORNE & LITTLE
CHRYSANTHE IN COLOR 2;
LINEN, COTTON
page 154

HIGHLAND COURT
ISABELLE IN TANGERINE; LINEN
page 160

GALBRAITH & PAUL
FLOWER POWER IN PINK;
LINEN
page 168

GALBRAITH & PAUL
PIZZELLE IN BABY BLUE; LINEN
page 168

KRAVET
GRACE IN PERIDOT; VISCOSE,
POLYESTER, SILK
page 171

FABRIC SWATCHES

FLOWERS AND FOLIAGE

PETER FASANO, LTD.
CAMP LEAVES; LINEN
page 172

WAVERLY
ROLLING MEADOW IN
CHAMBRAY; LINEN, RAYON
page 176

**TRAVERS THROUGH
ZIMMER + ROHDE**
OAKLEAVES IN BLUE; LINEN
page 176

RAOUL TEXTILES
PALOMA IN DELFT;
OYSTER LINEN
page 178

RAOUL TEXTILES
ANANAS IN CIEL; OYSTER LINEN
page 178

KRAVET
NATCHEZ IN SPICE;
RAYON, COTTON
page 191

COWTAN & TOUT
RAPHAELLO 10817-03 IN
DELFT; LINEN, COTTON
page 199

RAOUL TEXTILES
OCEAN FLOWERS (420N84) IN
PIMENTO; NATURAL LINEN
page 199

LES INDIENNES
ELISE IN OLIVE; COTTON
page 202

FABRIC SWATCHES

FLOWERS AND FOLIAGE

RAOUL TEXTILES
PHILIP IN CARDAMON;
NATURAL LINEN
page 202

**NEISHA CROSLAND
THROUGH STARK FABRIC**
BERRY FLOWER IN LEMON CURD;
COTTON | page 202

RAOUL TEXTILES
PASHA IN DELFT; OYSTER LINEN
page 204

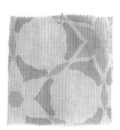

VANDERHURD
STELLAR 4 IN GREY AND
CHARTREUSE; NATURAL LINEN
page 210

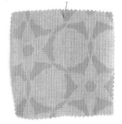

VANDERHURD
FLOWER STENCIL 5 IN
CHARTREUSE; NATURAL LINEN
page 210

**JASPER THROUGH
MICHAEL S. SMITH**
REMY 1515 IN BLUE; HEMP
page 212

**JASPER THROUGH
MICHAEL S. SMITH**
JAMMU IN SAFFRON; LINEN
page 214

SCHUMACHER
HOT HOUSE FLOWERS IN
MINERAL; LINEN
page 218

DONGHIA
OAHU IN LIGHT BLUE/BLUE;
ACRYLIC
page 220

FABRIC SWATCHES

PAISLEYS

SCHUMACHER
ABAZA RESIST IN INDIGO;
LINEN, COTTON
page 20

**OSCAR DE LA RENTA
FOR FONTHILL THROUGH
STARK FABRIC**
JAIPUR CREST IN BROWN; COTTON
page 32

TYLERGRAPHIC
GRANADA IN PINK; LINEN
page 54

**ROSE TARLOW
MELROSE HOUSE**
MONTAGUE IN SKY; HEMP LINEN
page 72

CLARENCE HOUSE
RAJASTHAN IN RED/BROWN;
COTTON, POLYESTER
page 87

**ALEXANDER JULIAN
THROUGH STOUT**
DISTINCTION IN DOMINO; SILK
page 94

**BEACON HILL THROUGH
ROBERT ALLEN**
DOVER IN PAPRIKA; COTTON,
POLYESTER | page 112

CLARENCE HOUSE
LA MALCONTENTA IN YELLOW/
BROWN; VISCOSE
page 130

DONGHIA
VICTORIA IN ASTER; RAYON,
COTTON | page 160

FABRIC SWATCHES

PAISLEYS

PETER DUNHAM TEXTILES
KASHMIR PAISLEY IN RED/BLUE; LINEN | pages 165, 187

RAOUL TEXTILES
SCROLL PAISLEY IN MAJOLICA; OYSTER LINEN
pages 178, 204, 222

PETER DUNHAM TEXTILES
SAMARKAND IN BLUE/RED; LINEN
page 186

BARCLAY BUTERA THROUGH KRAVET
CARREY IN BRICK; LINEN, SILK
page 194

QUADRILLE WALLPAPERS & FABRICS, INC.
NOTTINGHAM IN TAN; VISCOSE, ACRYLIC | page 196

LES INDIENNES
LA REINE IN OLIVE; COTTON
page 202

JOHN ROBSHAW
CINDE IN MONSOON; LINEN, COTTON | page 210

JASPER THROUGH MICHAEL S. SMITH
KASHMIR IN SAFFRON; HEMP
page 214

RAOUL TEXTILES
SARI IN SAFFRON; OYSTER LINEN
page 222

FABRIC SWATCHES

SCENICS AND TOILES

DONGHIA
SHANGRI-LA IN
JACARANDA/BROWN; LINEN
page 19

**BRAQUENIE THROUGH
PIERRE FREY**
TRAVAUX DE LA MANUFACTURE IN
BLEU; COTTON | page 22

PIERRE FREY
HONG KONG POSITIF IN
LAQUE; COTTON
page 22

LEE JOFA
FOLIE CHINOISE IN ROSE; COTTON
page 30

OLD WORLD WEAVERS
VOYAGE EN CHINE IN BLACK;
COTTON, LINEN
page 83

**MULBERRY HOME
THROUGH LEE JOFA**
PARISIAN SCENE IN BLACK; LINEN,
COTTON | page 94

SCALAMANDRÉ
PING IN COFFEE; LINEN
page 196

FABRIC SWATCHES

ANIMALS AND INSECTS

STROHEIM & ROMANN
STANLEY MATELASSÉ IN IVORY
(8284B-0014); COTTON
page 19

**PIERRE DEUX
THROUGH KRAVET**
BASSECOUR IN FRAMBOISE;
COTTON, NYLON, POLYESTER
page 24

**GREY WATKINS
THROUGH STARK FABRIC**
CHANTICLEER IN CHARCOAL;
COTTON, LINEN | page 24

THIBAUT
FISHBOWL IN WHITE; COTTON
page 120

LEE JOFA
INSECARE WEAVE IN CLOVER;
COTTON, RAYON
page 121

**MURIEL BRANDOLINI
THROUGH HOLLAND
& SHERRY**
WHITE NO. 5; INDIAN COTTON
page 180

FABRIC SWATCHES

PLAIDS AND CHECKS

PLACE TEXTILES
BANTRY CHECK IN HICKORY;
WOOL, NYLON
page 23

**T4 FABRICS THROUGH
QRNER STR**
HOUNDSTOOTH IN MIDNIGHT
BLUE; COTTON, LINEN
page 23

NANCY CORZINE
TRAFFIC IN OCEAN; SILK
page 46

**ROSE CUMMING THROUGH
DESSIN FOURNIR**
SILK PLAID IN RUBY; SILK
page 55

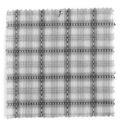

COWTAN & TOUT
MARCO CHECK IN ROSE;
RAYON, COTTON
page 55

SCALAMANDRÉ
MARA VISTA IN CORNFLOWER
BLUE & CREAM; VISCOSE, LINEN
page 56

BRUNSCHWIG & FILS
PAOLA IN PEPPER RED; SILK
TAFFETA | page 64

LEE JOFA
BELLA TAFFETA PLAID IN CHERRY;
SILK TAFFETA
page 67

ROGERS & GOFFIGON
MANCHESTER IN BLACK
STRAP; LINEN | page 80

FABRIC SWATCHES

PLAIDS AND CHECKS

LEE JOFA
CECIL WOOL PLAID IN
ROSEWOOD; WOOL
page 87

**OLD WORLD WEAVERS
THROUGH STARK FABRIC**
GARBO IN GRAPHITE; VISCOSE
BLEND | page 95

TYLER HALL
SUMMER PICNIC IN
WHEAT/GRASS; COTTON, LINEN
page 152

BARCLAY BUTERA HOME
ABSTRACT IN CREAM AND
BROWN; COTTON SLUB DUCK
page 171

LULU DK
WELLINGTON IN CHOCOLATE;
LINEN, VISCOSE
page 180

FABRIC SWATCHES

STRIPES

**THE ALEXA HAMPTON
COLLECTION THROUGH
KRAVET COUTURE**
GREEK KEY STRIPE IN GOLDEN
MERLOT (22285-419); SILK
TAFFETA | page 19

SCALAMANDRÉ
PROVINCE IN PALE BLUE
AND PEACH; SILK TAFFETA
page 30

**NINA CAMPBELL
THROUGH OSBORNE
& LITTLE** | VOLUTA STRIPE
IN COLOR 03; VISCOSE BLEND
page 39

KRAVET
SILK RIB STRIPE (9135-1615)
IN SPA; SILK
page 49

**JANE CHURCHILL
THROUGH COWTAN & TOUT**
TALPA STRIPE IN BLUE AND CREAM;
LINEN, COTTON, NYLON
page 50

TYLERGRAPHIC
POMPEII STRIPE IN
LE CIRQUE; LINEN
page 55

NANCY CORZINE
AMAGANSET STRIPE IN
BLUSH; LINEN
page 55

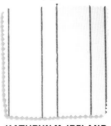

KATHRYN M. IRELAND
STRIPED SHEER IN RED; LINEN
page 62

**WILLIAM YEOWARD
THROUGH OSBORNE
& LITTLE**
KOTHI IN OLD ROSE; COTTON
page 67

FABRIC SWATCHES

STRIPES

ROGERS & GOFFIGON
DREAMCOAT IN RUBEN; LINEN
page 70

BRUNSCHWIG & FILS
JULIENNE IN STRIPE; TAFFETA
page 72

SCHUMACHER
GABRIELLE EMBROIDERY;
SILK, VISCOSE
page 79

ROGERS & GOFFIGON
TICKING IN VIRGINIA; COTTON
page 87

**OLD WORLD WEAVERS
THROUGH STARK FABRIC**
STRIÉ VELVET IN CRÈME; COTTON
VELVET | page 87

**GREY WATKINS THROUGH
STARK FABRIC**
RIVIERA STRIPE IN CANNES
GREEN; SILK, WOOL | page 88

RALPH LAUREN HOME
CRANE RIDGE TICKING IN
BLUE; LINEN
page 91

JOHN HUTTON TEXTILES
MOBY DICK IN MOODY BLUES;
VISCOSE, COTTON
page 103

**HODSOLL MCKENZIE
THROUGH ZIMMER + ROHDE**
REGENCY STRIPE IN 503;
SILK | page 104

FABRIC SWATCHES

STRIPES

ROGERS & GOFFIGON
PARRAMORE ISLAND IN
RED; LINEN
page 115

BRUNSCHWIG & FILS
MADHYA WOVEN STRIPE IN ROSE/
PISTACHIO; COTTON, ACRYLIC
page 122

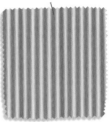

RALPH LAUREN HOME
CENTERVILLE TICKING IN LIGHT
BLUE; COTTON
page 125

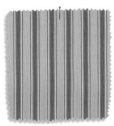

NORBAR
TOBAY IN SKY; COTTON
page 125

RALPH LAUREN HOME
RYAN STRIPE; COTTON
page 129

PINE CONE HILL
STARBOARD TICKING;
COTTON TWILL
page 129

**JANE CHURCHILL THROUGH
COWTAN & TOUT**
SAIL MULTI STRIPE IN BLUE; COTTON
page 133

T4 FABRICS
ALPHA STRIPE; COTTON, LINEN
page 136

**NORTHCROFT THROUGH
TODD ALEXANDER
ROMANO**
FAIDHERBE IN CANTON; COTTON,
POLYESTER | page 137

FABRIC SWATCHES

STRIPES

**MANUEL CANOVAS
THROUGH COWTAN & TOUT**
ELOI IN FRAISE; COTTON
page 144

CARLETON V
KILLISNOO IN PEAR;
COTTON, LINEN
page 152

CARLETON V
SOPHIE SHEER IN LIME; LINEN
page 153

LEE JOFA
RICAMO STRIPE IN SEASIDE;
LINEN, COTTON, NYLON
page 162

PETER DUNHAM TEXTILES
MATTRESS TICKING IN
PALE INDIGO; LINEN
page 165

KATHRYN M. IRELAND
TONAL TICKING IN GREEN; HEMP
page 176

**CAROLINA IRVING
TEXTILES**
PATMOS STRIPE IN PARSLEY;
HEMP | page 177

JANE SHELTON
LADDER STRIPE IN BROWN;
COTTON
page 177

**CAROLINA IRVING
TEXTILES**
PATMOS STRIPE IN POMPEII;
HEMP | page 187

FABRIC SWATCHES

STRIPES

**BARCLAY BUTERA
THROUGH KRAVET**
ENNOBLED IN LANTERN RED;
VISCOSE, COTTON
page 195

**SANDERSON
THROUGH ZOFFANY**
PINSTRIPE; LINEN BLEND
page 196

LULU DK
CHANT REVERSE IN ROYAL BLUE;
LINEN, COTTON
page 204

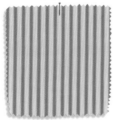

CARLETON V
WALLIS TICKING IN
GRASS; COTTON
page 207

SCHUMACHER
BAGAN IN BISCUIT; LINEN, SILK
page 219

RALPH LAUREN HOME
COASTAL STRIPE IN YELLOW
AND WHITE; COTTON
page 222

FABRIC SWATCHES

DOTS

FORTUNY
TAPA IN BROWN AND WARM
WHITE; COTTON
page 39

**ANNIE SELKE HOME
THROUGH CALICO
CORNERS**
SEEMA IN BLUEMARINE;
COTTON | page 43

TYLER HALL
CASA DI WHITNEY IN LINEN;
COTTON, VISCOSE, ACRYLIC
page 78

**CHINA SEAS THROUGH
QUADRILLE WALLPAPERS
& FABRICS, INC.**
GINZA IN BROWN, CAMEL, AQUA
ON WHITE; LINEN | page 136

LEE JOFA
TWISTER PRINT IN SKY AND
TANG; LINEN, COTTON, NYLON
page 162

PETER FASANO, LTD.
DOTTY; LINEN
page 173

JED JOHNSON HOME
MEDALLION IN IMPERIAL;
COTTON, LINEN
page 187

RAOUL TEXTILES
LIMOGES IN CIEL; OYSTER LINEN
page 204

VANDERHURD
DAISY CHAIN 17 IN SILVER AND
CHARTREUSE; CHANDERI
page 210

FABRIC SWATCHES

STYLIZED GEOMETRICS

DONGHIA
SUZANI IN PINK PASSION;
VISCOSE, SILK, POLYESTER
page 25

**CHINA SEAS THROUGH
QUADRILLE WALLPAPERS
& FABRICS, INC.**
SIGOURNEY IN JUNGLE GREEN ON
WHITE; LINEN, COTTON | page 25

LEE JOFA
HAMMOND IN OLIVE; VISCOSE,
COTTON | page 31

HIGHLAND COURT
ROBIN'S EGG IN BLUE ICE;
POLYESTER, VISCOSE
page 48

**KATE GABRIEL THROUGH
A.M. COLLECTIONS**
ARABESQUE IN FOG; LINEN
page 54

KATHRYN M. IRELAND
GRAHAM IN RED; HEMP LINEN
page 63

BRUNSCHWIG & FILS
LA MER (89756-147) IN POMPEIAN
RED; COTTON, VISCOSE,
POLYAMIDE | page 64

SCHUMACHER
DURANCE EMBROIDERY IN MINERAL;
LINEN, COTTON, POLYESTER
page 78

LULU DK
MADISON IN DRIFTWOOD;
ACRYLIC | page 96

FABRIC SWATCHES

STYLIZED GEOMETRICS

**THOMAS O'BRIEN
THROUGH LEE JOFA**
MOROCCO CHENILLE IN REEF;
RAYON, POLYESTER, COTTON
page 110

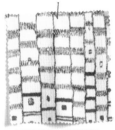

**THOMAS O'BRIEN
THROUGH LEE JOFA**
CALLIOPE IN OCHRE; SILK
page 110

FORTUNY
MELILLA IN INDIGO BLUE
AND SILVERY GOLD; COTTON
page 110

**THOMAS O'BRIEN
THROUGH LEE JOFA**
TAMORA WEAVE IN AEGEAN;
RAYON, COTTON | page 111

RAOUL TEXTILES
VIZCAYA IN CELERY; OYSTER LINEN
page 138

RAOUL TEXTILES
GRANADA IN ROBIN'S EGG;
NATURAL LINEN
page 138

**ALAN CAMPBELL THROUGH
QUADRILLE WALLPAPERS
& FABRICS, INC.**
ZIG ZAG AC (302-18) IN NAVY ON
TINT; LINEN, COTTON | page 149

CARLETON V
MALIBU IN MANGO; LINEN,
COTTON | page 153

ZOFFANY
MAZE IN BLUE; COTTON, LINEN
page 157

FABRIC SWATCHES

STYLIZED GEOMETRICS

HIGHLAND COURT
INTAGLIO IN TANGERINE;
RAYON, COTTON
page 160

HIGHLAND COURT
LABYRINTO IN PERSIMMON; RAYON
page 160

GALBRAITH & PAUL
MOUNTAINS IN KIWI;
OYSTER LINEN
page 168

SISTER PARISH DESIGN
THROUGH JOHN ROSSELLI
& ASSOCIATES, LTD.
TUCKERMAN IN GREEN; COTTON
TWILL | page 176

CHINA SEAS THROUGH
QUADRILLE WALLPAPERS
& FABRICS, INC.
ISLAND IKAT (6460-09) IN PALM
GREEN ON WHITE; LINEN | page 180

PETER DUNHAM TEXTILES
IKAT IN POMEGRANATE; LINEN
page 186

PETER DUNHAM
TEXTILES
STARBURST IN EAST; LINEN
page 187

MADELINE WEINRIB
DASHWOOD; SILK, COTTON
page 188

MADELINE WEINRIB
MU IN BROWN; SILK,
COTTON | page 188

FABRIC SWATCHES

STYLIZED GEOMETRICS

C&C MILANO THROUGH HOLLAND & SHERRY
PIENZA RAFANO IN BLUE NATURAL; LINEN | page 191

BARCLAY BUTERA THROUGH KRAVET
REALM IN CHINESE RED; LINEN, COTTON | page 194

SCHUMACHER
VAUGHAN CHENILLE IN PERSIMMON; ACRYLIC, POLYESTER, COTTON | page 194

JENNIFER ROBBINS TEXTILES
MIN IN MER WITH PLATINIUM; SILK, RAYON | page 203

MADELINE WEINRIB
DAPHNE IN HAZELNUT; SILK, COTTON | page 218

SCHUMACHER
BETWIXT IN CHARCOAL/ECRU; COTTON | page 218

SCHUMACHER
BLEECKER IN TWILIGHT; LINEN
page 219

RAOUL TEXTILES
CHUNARI IN BLUE WILLOW; NATURAL LINEN
page 222

FABRIC SWATCHES

ABSTRACTS AND ANIMAL SKINS

CELERIE II COLLECTION THROUGH VALTEKZ
RATTLESNAKE IN NATURAL; FAUX LEATHER | page 18

TRAVERS THROUGH ZIMMER + ROHDE
GRAMMONT (107133) IN LINEN; LINEN | page 40

CLARENCE HOUSE
MATISSE IN BLACK; COTTON
page 99

ROBERT ALLEN
ELEMENTS IN SEA; RAYON, POLYESTER
page 102

SCALAMANDRÉ
LEOPARDO IN IVORY, GOLD, AND BLACK; SILK VELVET
page 112

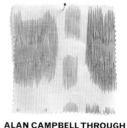

ALAN CAMPBELL THROUGH QUADRILLE WALLPAPERS & FABRICS, INC.
CINTRA IN TANGERINE/JUNGLE GREEN ON TINT; LINEN | page 120

DESIGNERS GUILD THROUGH OSBORNE & LITTLE
PEAWEED IN INDIGO; COTTON
page 133

JANE SHELTON
VERMICELLI SQUARE IN BLUE; LINEN | page 136

CHINA SEAS THROUGH QUADRILLE WALLPAPERS & FABRICS, INC.
NAIROBI IN JUNGLE GREEN ON TINT; LINEN, COTTON | page 139

FABRIC SWATCHES

ABSTRACTS AND ANIMAL SKINS

CHINA SEAS THROUGH QUADRILLE WALLPAPERS & FABRICS, INC.
RIO IN GREEN GRASS ON WHITE; LINEN, COTTON | page 140

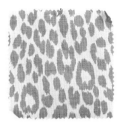

RAOUL TEXTILES
LEOPARD IN OLIVINE; IVORY LINEN
page 142

BRUNSCHWIG & FILS
VANESSA'S FOLLY COTTON PRINT IN TURQUOISE; COTTON
page 145

SCALAMANDRÉ
OASIS IN IVORY, BLUE, AND YELLOW; LINEN, POLYESTER
page 203

FABRIC SWATCHES

DAMASK

NANCY CORZINE
CORNUCOPIA IN GOLD; SILK
page 20

CHELSEA EDITIONS
FRENCH KNOT (2011-01) IN
CREAM; LINEN, COTTON
page 35

**COLONY COLLECTION
THROUGH SCALAMANDRÉ**
RONDO IN LINEN AND STRAW;
COTTON, VISCOSE, SILK | page 38

NANCY CORZINE
NATASHA IN AQUA; SILK, LINEN
page 46

TYLERGRAPHIC
ROSE DU ROI IN PLATINUM;
COTTON, SILK
page 54

STROHEIM & ROMANN
TANTI FIGURED WOVEN IN AQUA;
COTTON, VISCOSE, LINEN
page 79

SCHUMACHER
PONT ROYAL DAMASK IN
MINERAL; LINEN, COTTON
page 79

SCHUMACHER
LUCIENNE DAMASK IN PERIDOT;
SILK | page 88

DOGWOOD
DAVENHAM IN BISCUIT; LINEN,
VISCOSE
page 104

FABRIC SWATCHES

DAMASK

J. ROBERT SCOTT
MATIGNON IN DOVE; SILK DAMASK
page 107

**CLASSIC CLOTH
THROUGH DESSIN
FOURNIR**
MATELASSÉ DAMASK IN MORTAR;
COTTON, WOOL, SILK | page 107

**NORTHCROFT THROUGH
TODD ALEXANDER
ROMANO**
CARNOT IN CANTON; COTTON,
POLYESTER | page 137

FABRIC SWATCHES

SOLIDS AND SUBTLE PATTERNS

ROGERS & GOFFIGON
SHAKER IN BLITHE (92509-05);
LINEN | page 18

**LELIEVRE THROUGH
OLD WORLD WEAVERS**
VENUS DOT IN AZALEE
(H007470044); SILK BLEND
page 19

**LARSEN THROUGH
COWTAN & TOUT**
SERENITY IN AZURE; SILK, WOOL
page 30

LEE JOFA
GLAZED SILK IN OCEAN; COTTON,
SILK | page 30

**LARSEN THROUGH
COWTAN & TOUT**
CANTON VELVET IN AZURE; SILK,
COTTON, WOOL | page 31

ROGERS & GOFFIGON
CODA IN WISK; NYLON, COTTON
page 31

LEE JOFA
COVINGTON IN ROSE; COTTON,
VISCOSE
page 31

BRUNSCHWIG & FILS
NORFOLK STRIÉ TEXTURE IN LEAF
GREEN; COTTON, RAYON
page 32

**C&C MILANO THROUGH
HOLLAND & SHERRY**
000332 IN GREY-BLUE/IVORY;
LINEN | page 35

FABRIC SWATCHES

SOLIDS AND SUBTLE PATTERNS

JANE CHURCHILL THROUGH COWTAN & TOUT
SHELLEY IN CREAM; COTTON, VISCOSE, LINEN | page 35

LELIEVRE THROUGH STARK FABRIC
DIAPASON IN ANIS; POLYESTER
page 38

NINA CAMPBELL THROUGH OSBORNE & LITTLE
GIVERNY VELVET IN COLOR 03; COTTON, VISCOSE | page 38

NINA CAMPBELL THROUGH OSBORNE & LITTLE
AMISI IN COLOR 03; VISCOSE BLEND | page 39

PIERRE FREY
TEDDY IN OLIVE; MOHAIR, COTTON | page 39

GREAT PLAINS THROUGH HOLLY HUNT
SUMMER CLOTH IN SEASPRAY; LINEN, COTTON | page 40

ANNIE SELKE HOME THROUGH CALICO CORNERS
TARA IN CHOCOLATE; COTTON
page 43

NANCY CORZINE
ZHANDARA IN ROBIN'S EGG; SILK
page 46

NANCY CORZINE
CHINÉE IN PEARL/BLONDE; SILK
page 46

FABRIC SWATCHES

SOLIDS AND SUBTLE PATTERNS

ROGERS & GOFFIGON
SOUSSOUS IN TARN; LINEN,
SILK, COTTON
page 47

NANCY CORZINE
DIAMANTÉ IN PALE TEA; SILK
page 47

ROGERS & GOFFIGON
LAPIDARY IN LAGOON; LINEN, SILK
page 47

JANE SHELTON
MADISON LINEN IN BLUE; LINEN
page 56

SCHUMACHER
STONE TEXTURE IN ECRU; COTTON
page 59

KATHRYN M. IRELAND
BOUCLE IN RED; COTTON, RAYON
page 62

CHELSEA EDITIONS
QUEEN ANNE VINE IN WHITE;
LINEN, COTTON
page 62

FABRICUT
HOLMES IN PEAR; LINEN, COTTON
page 67

ROGERS & GOFFIGON
PELOTON IN BREAKAWAY; LINEN
page 70

FABRIC SWATCHES

SOLIDS AND SUBTLE PATTERNS

TWILL TEXTILES
GOOSEYE IN LAKE; COTTON, LINEN
page 70

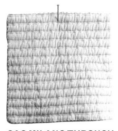

**C&C MILANO THROUGH
HOLLAND & SHERRY**
GIGLIO IN WHITE ISA; COTTON
page 70

ROGERS & GOFFIGON
BIARRITZ IN FOUNTAIN; COTTON,
CASHMERE
page 71

ROGERS & GOFFIGON
BECHAMEL IN MANTIS; WOOL
page 71

EDELMAN LEATHER
LUXE CALF IN WATERFALLS;
LEATHER
page 71

ROGERS & GOFFIGON
HORSEHAIR I IN BIRDSTONE;
HORSEHAIR, LINEN, SISAL
page 71

ROGERS & GOFFIGON
NEVIS IN MALT; LINEN, COTTON
page 75

CLAREMONT
TOILE CHENONCEAU IN CRÈME;
RAYON, WOOL, SILK
page 78

**HODSOLL MCKENZIE
THROUGH ZIMMER + ROHDE**
SILK LINEN STRIÉ IN 955; LINEN,
SILK | page 79

FABRIC SWATCHES

SOLIDS AND SUBTLE PATTERNS

ROGERS & GOFFIGON
COUNTRY CLOTH IN MOREL;
LINEN | page 80

ROGERS & GOFFIGON
SHAKER IN WHEAT; LINEN
page 81

JOSEPH NOBLE
LUXURIOUS IN ASH; COTTON
VELVET | page 83

SCHUMACHER
GAINSBOROUGH IN CHOCOLATE;
COTTON VELVET
page 86

ROGERS & GOFFIGON
BECHAMEL IN TSUNAMI; WOOL
page 86

**C&C MILANO THROUGH
HOLLAND & SHERRY**
MAREMMA IN DARK RED; LINEN
page 86

BRUNSCHWIG & FILS
SCALA METISSE IN 910; COTTON,
LINEN | page 90

**COLEFAX AND FOWLER
THROUGH COWTAN & TOUT**
CHILTERN BOUCLE IN BLUE, CREAM;
COTTON | page 90

CLARENCE HOUSE
VELOURS GASCOGNE IN PIVOINE;
COTTON, LINEN, CUT VELVET
page 94

FABRIC SWATCHES

SOLIDS AND SUBTLE PATTERNS

EDELMAN LEATHER
BASKET WEAVE IN SWAMP;
LEATHER | page 95

EDELMAN LEATHER
CAVALLINI IN PEARL GREY;
COWHIDE | page 95

**MISSONI THROUGH
STARK FABRIC**
ZERMATT IN BLACK AND WHITE;
COTTON | page 95

CLARENCE HOUSE
COTTON VELVET IN BURGHUNDY;
COTTON | page 98

CALICO CORNERS
CRANSTON IN IVORY; COTTON
page 99

ROBERT ALLEN
NATURES WEB IN MICA;
POLYESTER
page 102

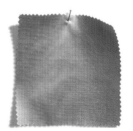

JOHN HUTTON TEXTILES
PRECIOUS METAL IN PLATNIUM;
SILK, LUREX
page 102

**RUBELLI THROUGH BER-
GAMO FABRICS**
PANFORTE IN COLOR 9; VISCOSE
BLEND | page 103

ROBERT ALLEN
ENTHUSIAST IN WATER;
VISCOSE BLEND
page 103

FABRIC SWATCHES

SOLIDS AND SUBTLE PATTERNS

EDELMAN LEATHER
SHAGREEN IN CAVIAR; LEATHER
page 103

**CLASSIC CLOTH
THROUGH DESSIN
FOURNIR**
AUBUSSON IN GREY GOOSE;
COTTON, SILK | page 107

**MULBERRY HOME
THROUGH LEE JOFA**
STEED CHENILLE IN SAND;
VISCOSE, COTTON | page 111

SCALAMANDRÉ
CORKE LODGE IN GOLD;
SILK VELVET
page 111

ROGERS & GOFFIGON
RONDO IN RHYME; LINEN
page 111

KRAVET
MINUET IN HERITAGE GREEN;
SILK VELVET
page 112

GRETCHEN BELLINGER
PASHA IN CLARIFIED BUTTER;
LINEN, LINEN VELVET
page 115

**FONTHILL THROUGH
STARK FABRIC**
CHELSEA STRIÉ VELVET IN GLADE;
COTTON VELVET | page 115

PIERRE DEUX
OTTOMAN IN ORANGE; COTTON,
POLYESTER
page 121

FABRIC SWATCHES

SOLIDS AND SUBTLE PATTERNS

BRUNSCHWIG & FILS
CHANCELLOR STRIÉ IN JADE;
VISCOSE, COTTON BLEND
page 121

PIERRE FREY
BEAUBOURG 2190 IN DRAGEE 258;
TREVIRA CS
page 125

RALPH LAUREN HOME
MONTGOMERY HERRINGBONE
IN FLAX; LINEN, COTTON
page 128

**SEACLOTH THROUGH LEE
JOFA**
WOVEN SOLID IN MIDNIGHT;
COTTON | page 128

**SEACLOTH THROUGH
LEE JOFA**
SOLID IN PARCHMENT; COTTON,
LINEN | page 129

**LARSEN THROUGH
COWTAN & TOUT**
CINEMA IN KOALA; MOHAIR,
COTTON | page 130

**NORTHCROFT THROUGH
TODD ALEXANDER
ROMANO**
ROCHELLE IN AQUA; COTTON
page 137

ROGERS & GOFFIGON
FIORELLA IN VAN DYKE; LINEN,
SILK | page 137

BRUNSCHWIG & FILS
GAUGUIN LINEN TEXTURE
(89588-434) IN AVOCADO; LINEN
page 138

FABRIC SWATCHES

SOLIDS AND SUBTLE PATTERNS

PIERRE FREY
SHABBY IN ABSINTHE; LINEN
page 141

**MANUEL CANOVAS
THROUGH COWTAN
& TOUT**
COTTON CLUB II IN FRAMBOISE;
COTTON | page 144

**MANUEL CANOVAS
THROUGH COWTAN
& TOUT**
INDOCHINE IN CERISE; VISCOSE,
COTTON | page 145

**MANUEL CANOVAS
THROUGH COWTAN
& TOUT**
BRASILIA IN ANIS; VISCOSE,
LINEN | page 145

**MANUEL CANOVAS
THROUGH COWTAN
& TOUT**
MAROQUIN IN TILLEUL; COTTON,
VISCOSE | page 145

**JANE CHURCHILL
THROUGH COWTAN
& TOUT**
FLORIAN PLAIN IN DARK
BLUE; COTTON | page 148

CARLETON V
SIENA IN GREEN; COTTON,
VISCOSE, LINEN, SILK
page 152

HINSON & CO.
HINSON SUEDE IN SALMON;
MICROFIBER
page 153

**BASSETT MCNAB
COMPANY**
JUMPER IN SNAPDRAGON; RAYON,
POLYESTER, NYLON | page 153

FABRIC SWATCHES

SOLIDS AND SUBTLE PATTERNS

ROMO
LEONI IN ICE BLUE; LINEN BLEND
page 157

ARCHITEX
MANFRED IN ESPRESSO;
COTTON, WOOL
page 161

HIGHLAND COURT
PACHA IN ABSINTHE; COTTON,
RAYON | page 161

HIGHLAND COURT
VENETO IN GRAPHITE;
ALPACA VELVET
page 161

BRENTANO FABRICS
MUKHMAL IN MOLASSES;
ACRYLIC, POLYESTER, OLEFIN
page 161

NOBILIS
ATLAS (46428) IN CORAL; LINEN
page 162

**OLD WORLD WEAVERS
THROUGH STARK FABRIC**
RAVENNE FLAME STITCH IN
AMARANTE; COTTON, SILK,
ACRYLIC BLEND | page 168

SCHUMACHER
NE PLUS ULTRA IN CADET;
COTTON VELVET
page 169

ROMO
LINARA IN PERIDOT; COTTON,
LINEN | page 169

FABRIC SWATCHES

SOLIDS AND SUBTLE PATTERNS

SANDRA JORDAN
PRIMA ALPACA IN PARCELA;
ALPACA | page 169

**LELIEVRE THROUGH
STARK FABRIC**
LE JAZZ IN CORAIL; POLYESTER
page 169

ROMO
LINARA IN ELECTRIC BLUE;
COTTON, LINEN
page 172

CLARENCE HOUSE
LIDO IN OFF-WHITE; VISCOSE,
LINEN | page 177

**SISTER PARISH
DESIGN THROUGH
JOHN ROSSELLI &
ASSOCIATES, LTD.**
LOGAN IN GREEN; COTTON | page 177

KATHRYN M. IRELAND
WOVEN IN RED; LINEN
page 186

**JASPER THROUGH MI-
CHAEL S. SMITH**
GAVLE IN BLUE; LINEN
page 186

LIBECO-LAGAE
P533 IN ARABICA; BELGIAN
LINEN | page 191

KRAVET
SILK SKIN IN GARNET; LINEN,
SILK, RAYON
page 194

FABRIC SWATCHES

SOLIDS AND SUBTLE PATTERNS

BARCLAY BUTERA HOME
ABSOLUTE IN TOMATO; LEATHER
page 195

RALPH LAUREN HOME
WESTWOOD IN RATTAN; RAYON,
NYLON, POLYESTER
page 195

RALPH LAUREN HOME
NIGEL IN HARVEST; MOHAIR
page 195

DEDAR
BOUTIS IN EBANO; COTTON, NYLON
page 203

HOLLAND & SHERRY
CHAMONIX IN WHITE; WOOL
page 203

BRUNSCHWIG & FILS
BOTTICELLI IN LICHEN; COTTON,
VELVET | page 207

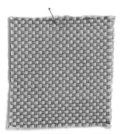

CHAPAS TEXTILES
THEBES IN CACTUS; COTTON
page 211

CLAREMONT
SERGE ANTIQUE IN COLOR 92;
RAYON, COTTON
page 211

JERRY PAIR LEATHER
HOOF IT IN COGNAC; LEATHER
page 211

FABRIC SWATCHES

SOLIDS AND SUBTLE PATTERNS

**GEORGE SPENCER
DESIGNS THROUGH
CLAREMONT**
UNO IN NATURAL; LINEN | page 211

**TRAVERS THROUGH
ZIMMER + ROHDE**
RENISHAW (400143) IN MELON;
VISCOSE, LINEN | page 212

KRAVET
8590 IN COLOR I; POLYACRYLIC
BLEND | page 218

VALTEKZ
MORAY IN POMEGRANATE;
PVC, COTTON
page 219

SCHUMACHER
GLIMMER IN MINERAL; ACRYLIC,
COTTON BLEND
page 219

DONGHIA
LANAI IN BLUE; ACRYLIC
page 220

DESIGNER INDEX

FABRIC INDEX

PHOTO CREDITS

Christopher Baker: 73

John Gould Bessler: 51, 114, 131, 156, 173

James Carrière: 97, 155, 182 (bottom)

Reed Davis: 189, 215

Douglas Friedman: 12

Tria Giovan: 124, 183, 197

Gridley + Graves: 113

Ken Hayden: 117, 170

Thibault Jeanson: 74, 89

John Kernick: 42, 49

Francesco Lagnese: 11, 33, 206

Thomas Loof: 106

McCaffety: 82

Laura Moss: 5, 179, 182 (top)

Ngoc Minh Ngo: 66, 132, 163, 181, 190, 205, 223

Victoria Pearson: 9, 164

Eric Piasecki: 2, 57, 81, 91, 116 (top), 139

Jeremy Samuelson: 16 (bottom), 17, 41, 98, 116 (bottom), 141, 149

Nathan Schroder: 16 (top), 65, 105, 146

Simon Upton: 213

Mikkel Vang: 123

Dominique Vorillon: 198

Julian Wass: 34, 221

Luke White: 58

House Beautiful
COLORS YOU'LL LOVE

Based on **House Beautiful's** popular monthly
column, this handy guide is filled with more than
300 paint formulas that professional interior designers
have used successfully in their own rooms. It explains
why the colors work and where they work best. From
cheerful blues to adventurous reds, from soothing
lavenders to sunny yellows, the colors you'll live
with happily for years are right here.

House Beautiful
COLORS FOR YOUR HOME
300 DESIGNER FAVORITES

HEARST BOOKS
A Division of Sterling Publishing Co., Inc.

Have a comment about our books?
We'd love to hear from you. Email us at booklover@hearst.com.